Reviews

"*A Glimpse behind the Veil* by Richard Rowland is absolutely compelling. I laughed, and I cried. The author shares wonderfully moving stories about animals, illustrating their intelligence and spiritual connection to all. If you've ever doubted that animals have souls, you'll witness those doubts dissolve as you turn the pages in this delightful book. I strongly recommend that everyone read this once and then read it to their children. We have, as a people, for all too long ignored our duty to animals who only want to help us in our journey through life. I will be buying several copies to share with those close to me and suggest you do the same."

Eldon Taylor, PhD, *New York Times* best-selling author of *Choices and Illusions*, radio host of *Provocative Enlightenment*

"For a human to be loved by another animal is to receive one of the many blessings of the animal kingdom. To love an animal is to step into that kingdom of our origin, which is where our humility, empathy, and compassion evolve to define and refine our humanity with the promise of dignity and grace. *A Glimpse behind the Veil* helps us find our way and affirms the wisdom of an open heart."

Dr. Michael W. Fox, veterinarian, author of *Animals and Nature First*, www.drfoxonehealth.com

A Journey of the Heart Continues ...

"Take comfort in knowing that miracles are the norm. Sometimes we are blessed to experience their reality in ways we would never have believed, and sometimes we are only able to see them because we already believe.

"The miracles shared within the pages of *A Glimpse behind the Veil* are spiritual encounters that transcend the barriers people have established between humans and other species from the moment the gates of Eden closed behind the first of our kind. We forgot that animals were created to be our companions and that we were assigned the responsibility of caring for them. In return for exercising that privilege, we learn to communicate with them and to enjoy their calming, healing, humorous, life-changing presence, forming a heart-to-heart bond that needs no words to be understood. People and animals were designed to belong to each other, and both lives are changed for the better when our spirits connect.

"Richard D. Rowland is an excellent writer and an outstanding storyteller. The wonder of *A Glimpse behind the Veil* is that all these stories are true. The believer in magic and the stickler for facts will discover that the recipe for living a full life calls for healthy portions of both. We only need to silence those inner voices that suspect the supernatural, insisting that life exists no farther than what our eyes can see, to experience our own glimpse behind the veil."

A. C. Townsend, author of the Trinity Conspiracy series

"With his excellent storytelling ability, Rowland draws you in for a cozy conversation like a dear friend. For those seeking, his collection of stories offers enlightenment. For those hurting, it offers comfort. Rowland weaves tales from multiple people about multiple animals into a cohesive, easy-flowing web of inspiration. I laughed. I cried. And at the end of *A Glimpse behind the Veil*, I found myself encouraged, moved, and a bit closer to something beyond myself.

"Thank you for a reminder to see the miraculous!"

D. A. Lawson, author of *Of Dreams and Tragedies*
and the Second Chances series

"In his new book, author Richard D. Rowland takes us on a continuing journey of ourselves as valued companions of the human, animal, and spiritual worlds that he defines through a myriad of true stories providing substantial corroborative theories that help identify unobvious facts. We become believers in a proposition that all life in the universe has value and the ability to relate and communicate together once a higher level has been achieved in critical thought and spiritual meditations.

"The combined community of stories offered by the author and his many friends are more than anecdotal; they make believers out of those who want to be connected with something bigger than just their preawakened beliefs within the human regiment. In fact, it shifts your higher learning to attain convictions that we are one in the life of past, present, and future … and that our stories and spirits are everlasting.

"Richard D. Rowland is a true prospector of truth of life and purpose, enticing the reader to boldly peer behind the veil and find the questions that will lead to your enlightened soul.

"I found his book to be adventurous and daringly provocative!"

J. L. "Jim" Hodges, author of *Murder:*
Above Top, www.cowboyspeaks.com

"You immediately get pulled into Richard's world with the wonderful animals who surround him and those people he has interviewed for this book. I felt as if I were sitting across the table from him and we were having tea together, and he was sharing story after beautiful story with me. 'Man plans while God smiles,' he says. I cannot agree more. Animals really are old souls, and Richard tells us all we have to do is be open to the magic. He's right. Open yourself to this book, and let the magic in. It has been said that there is no such thing as a coincidence and everything happens for a reason. The same thing is true with every animal that comes into your life. There is a reason if you will open your mind to receive the message of peace, encouragement, and love."

Melanie Lee, author of *So You Want to Move to Maine?*

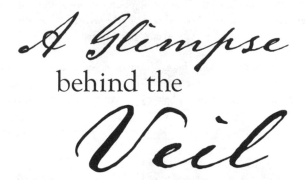

A Glimpse behind the Veil

Stories about the Human-Animal Connection

RICHARD D. ROWLAND

BALBOA.PRESS
A DIVISION OF HAY HOUSE

Balboa Press books may be ordered through booksellers or by contacting:

Balboa Press
A Division of Hay House
1663 Liberty Drive
Bloomington, IN 47403
www.balboapress.com
844-682-1282

Print information available on the last page.

ISBN: 978-1-9822-5553-4 (sc)
ISBN: 978-1-9822-5555-8 (hc)
ISBN: 978-1-9822-5554-1 (e)

Library of Congress Control Number: 2020918604

Balboa Press rev. date: 09/23/2020

This book is dedicated
to the animal kingdom and all
those within it who seek
nothing but our
company and understanding.
Through reading the words, may we find a new
level of thoughtful and peaceful coexistence.

Just for Today
let me take a step back from the human race
and place my focus solely upon the animal kingdom.
Allow me to hold them in hand, feel their energy,
warmth, and soak in their peace.
Let me learn to rest when tired and
eat when hungry.
Let me embrace the idea they just may
be old souls with much to teach
and open me to learn their wisdom.

R. D. Rowland

Acknowledgments

THIS IS THE PART WHERE I get to thank everyone who helped me to finish this project. If I did a complete job and mentioned everyone by name, the list would be longer than the book. Therefore, admittedly, this is an abbreviated list.

First and foremost, thanks to all the people who were willing to tell their stories publicly and allow me to tweak them to fit the book. Some were worried about people thinking they were crazy, but honestly, the people who are drawn to this book will believe just as the tellers of the tale do.

Thanks to my wonderful editor, Jeanne V. Benedict. The thanks are accompanied by an apology. Sorry about all the pronouns needing correction, and yes, I do use *that* a lot. I am working on it. I appreciate your skills with the English language, your organizational gifts, and your willingness to share them. To the readers, any mistakes you may find are mine and mine alone.

About twelve years ago, while scrolling through social media, I became a huge fan of Karen McGonigal-Coe, an artist from Alberta, Canada, who owns Karen Coe Fine Arts. Her works were captivating from the very beginning. The images looked as if you could walk into the paintings. Well, I was lucky enough to get Karen to agree to do the cover art for this project. I sent her a copy of the prepublished book to read, and then her vision took off. Her artistic eye saw images within the words she read, and she did what she does best. She created exactly what my imagination envisioned. Thank you, Karen.

I am very appreciative of those talented writers who willingly took time from their craft to not only read but also review this book. Your willingness helps me get the word out, drives interest in reading my books, and is a validation of my work. Thank you, Dr. Eldon Taylor, Dr. Michael Fox, Angela Townsend, D. A. Lawson, Jim Hodges, and Melanie Lee. Your collective friendships are safely guarded and often viewed in my life's treasure chest.

Most thank-you acknowledgements are easy to write. This one is tougher, as I fight for brevity while also struggling to contain the tears that want to come. I belong to a tribe of others who share a cancer diagnosis. We are a support system made up only of those who understand what we go through. Recently, one of our members gained her angel wings, but not before gifting the rest of us with smiles, laughter, and a strong belief in a continuing life. Shannon Borgel Holderfield passed on January 23, 2020. During one of our many marathon text sessions, she left me with some words that resonated with my soul, and I have quoted her many times since. "I can do this, and I will do it with grace and courage and bravery! My children are watching me handle this and it is my job to show them we don't collapse when the world pushes us! We rise to the challenge; some days we win, some days we lose! That's life." Thank you, Shannon, for bringing light, love, hope, and understanding to me on my darkest days. I will see you again one day. Without your support, this book might have remained but a thought.

Thank you to all those who read *Unspoken Messages* and wrote asking me when I would be coming out with a new book. In answer, I am coming out with a new book right now.

Thanks to my son for being a great human and teacher. It is nice when you don't have a head full of worries when thinking about your children. His help and proofreading skills went a long way toward bringing you the words you are about to read.

And finally, thank you to my wife, Jennifer. She not only put up with me disappearing for days on end as I sat behind a computer, writing and doing research, but she kept me fed, was my number-one proofreader, and came up with some super ideas for direction and organization. She was a steady hand when I was frustrated with things. She also pointed out I used the word *that* a lot and replaced many of them with words that worked better.

> If you can lie down at night, knowing in your
> heart that you made someone's day just a
> little bit better, you know you have had a good day.

Contents

Introduction

IT HAS LONG BEEN MY practice to study the introductions to every book I read. I actually see them as a road map for the book I am about to read, giving direction and insight to the coming journey with thought and word.

The journey you are about to embark on, contained within the pages of this book, began long ago when I received an initially devastating cancer diagnosis. This diagnosis came with an unsolicited death sentence of three years. I guess this is the point where I should tell you that it has now been twelve years. I also count the half years and will probably count quarter years if the timing is right. See, I am delighted with each day I get. It is not because I want to prove people wrong; it is merely that I have actually and finally learned to enjoy each day I am given. My focus has shifted to experiencing joy, love, and peace; learning; writing; the teachings of the animal kingdom; and living in the now.

Early in this dance I have had with cancer, I wrote a book titled *Unspoken Messages: Spiritual Lessons I Learned from Horses and Other Earthbound Souls*. It is a two-part book. In part one, there are ten stories of experiences I had with the animal kingdom. Part two's focus is how to navigate life with cancer. My focus here in this book goes back to part one of *Unspoken Messages*. Animals were the catalyst for change in me. I had to rethink life and all the magic that was previously hidden from me. Animals showed me things I didn't think possible, even when I witnessed them myself. It was a time of much-needed change in this old cowboy.

As I was going through this change, I thought I was the only one to see the miracles I found myself privy to. It wasn't until *Unspoken Messages* came out that I discovered many others have had experiences exactly like mine. People began writing me to tell me of their interactions with animals that bordered upon the unbelievable to those who still live in a science-based world. Some of the stories they told me differed from mine only in location and those present. It was around this time the idea for this book was born. The only question I was asking was whether there were enough magical experiences to fill a book. The answer was a resounding yes! As a matter of fact, I could fill books, not just *a* book, with incredible stories about the animal kingdom. Me? I have arrived at a place where I believe animals stand as nature's gifts to me. When I am in their presence, nothing else exists—not pain, sickness, elation, or excitement. Instead, it is a simple nothingness and everything at the same time.

A Glimpse behind the Veil is a book of stories about animals and the things they do that we mistakenly write off as coincidental. It mirrors my fervent belief that animals are far more evolved than we have been led to believe. See, like you, I was raised with a set of beliefs, but those beliefs belonged to someone else, and for most of my life, I embraced those beliefs as truth. It wasn't until my life was challenged by cancer that the veil thinned, and I was allowed a peek behind it. My conclusion is that maybe those who taught us didn't know the depth of soul possessed by the animal kingdom. All of them are magical and highly advanced sentient beings capable of showing us the truth about this universe, but we have to be open to see what they show. If we are closed, we will miss the message.

I was lucky to meet and interview people from all over the world about their experiences. Some stories may seem more powerful than others, but there are influential messages in each encounter, and they point to animals as a largely misunderstood part of our world. Some of the people who were interviewed or exchanged information via email wanted to keep their privacy. Names and locations have been changed in the book to honor those requests. Two things remain constant: each story remains true to the event, and I know the tellers of the tales.

Now it is time to turn the page and allow the journey to begin in earnest. I hope you get as much enjoyment from reading these stories as I did from talking to those who had the experiences and gave voice to their stories.

A Glance Backward

HAVE YOU EVER HEARD A horse person say, "This is a once-in-a-lifetime horse"? Well, I, for one, have uttered such a phrase before and, in all probability, will again. See, even at my rapidly advancing age, I am not yet through with having horses in my life and hope to never experience an existence without them.

This is a story about one of those horses—a once-in-a-lifetime horse. I have been lucky enough to have had several once-in-a-lifetime horses, but this is a story about one of the best, and the lessons he taught me are innumerable.

Some of you are familiar with this horse. His original story is told in the book *Unspoken Messages*. The title of his story is "Wild-Eyed and Laid Up." Those who have read it know the horse's name is Pal, and if you haven't yet read his story, get ready to meet the one and only goober, gomer, and trickster known as Pal.

A Recap of Old News

M Y WIFE, JENNIFER; SON, MATT; and I were the owners and operators of an equine facility about forty-some-odd miles south of Louisville, Kentucky, when we met Pal on one early fall day in 2007. He arrived at the stables with his longtime pasture mate, Sara. Their owners had chosen to board them at our stables. Both Pal and Sara came with some severe and challenging health issues. In fact, shortly after arriving, Sara developed bone cancer, broke her shoulder, and required help across the rainbow bridge.

Although saddened at the loss of his longtime friend, Pal had little choice but to carve out an existence at our farm, and he did it with a flair that was his alone. He had to make new friends and learn the local herd politics, pecking order, and many other things that would make his stay at our farm much more enjoyable. The biggest thing Pal had to learn and, at the same time, teach us was how to manage his worsening founder.

Founder, or laminitis, is a disease that affects the hooves of a horse. Many things can cause founder; normally, it is diet or stress related. Once a horse has foundered, he is foundered for life, and you must find a way to control it. The soft tissue (laminae) between the inner hoof wall and leg bones becomes inflamed and swells. The problem is there is nowhere for the swelling to go. Then the tissue that initially swelled dies and leaves an unstable foundation for the hooves. If it is a severe enough case of founder, the swelling causes the small bone (coffin bone) at the end of the leg to rotate. If the degree of rotation is too much, the bone can come out the bottom of the hoof. Any rotation of the coffin bone causes extreme discomfort for the horse when standing or trying to walk. Pal came to us with a severe case of founder and eye cancer. It certainly seemed our work was cut out for us. We chose to adopt Pal and agreed to take care of all his needs for the rest of his life. Failure was not an option. The eye cancer was taken care of in short order nutritionally, but the founder turned out to be a much steeper mountain to climb, filled with sheer walls and deep crevasses that would challenge every step forward we took.

In the years prior to Pal's story being published, we did everything in our power to find a way for him to enjoy a relatively pain-free existence, just as I promised him and myself we would. And we were relatively successful at times. The most magical day for us was when Pal returned to a level of health that allowed him to once again be ridden. That day was the point where the story in *Unspoken Messages* came to an end. It was also the day a new book began because the story continued and had so much more that needed to be told. Did we find a cure? Did we have to euthanize Pal? Did we find a way to make life enjoyable for him? Read on and find out.

You can't change what you refuse to face.

An Up-and-Down Existence

I've had the luxury of living a life where animals play a huge part in my everyday existence. I have also been around my (un)fair share of animals who have crossed over. Simple to say, but generally, we live longer than most of them and will be with them when they take their last breath. My love for animals is deep and unconditional. I would never let one suffer if death were imminent. That said, I also am one who believes animals will let me know if they are ready to get on the bridge. They will have a look in their eyes—one that would denote not resignation or fear as one might think but anticipation for what eventually comes for all. The apparent lack of fear is what has taught me the most about this dance with death that we all participate in daily. Hopefully, death is not at the forefront of our minds daily. It shouldn't be—that would be a little depressing. But no one can say he or she is unaware of this rhythmic dance in which we two-step through life.

It just so happens that I am one of those people who considers animals a bit more evolved than we humans, and I know they have much to teach me. I just wish I had paid attention to their lessons sooner in life. A lot of the late messages came from Pal. He would cycle in and out of severe bouts of founder. Every time we thought we had it beaten down, it would once again make its presence known. Sometimes we would go more than a year without a flare-up, and other times it was mere weeks. We would go to bed with Pal up and apparently feeling well and awake to find him lying in his stall, writhing in pain. Not one single time were we able to pinpoint the exact cause of the latest flare, and in the big picture, it may not have mattered. What did matter was finding the relief he sorely deserved. See, even with the intense pain, Pal never once told me he was ready to give up. Oh, to be sure, he asked for help, and he let me know how bad he hurt, but never once did he indicate he was ready to go. We were determined to continue the search for something to help him as long as he wanted to continue living.

Living large is one thing Pal did with gusto. He was, without doubt, the friendliest, most playful horse I have ever been around. He loved playing tag and hide-and-seek. He would poke you if you were not watching and then act like it wasn't him and rub his muzzle against anything that would scratch it for him. One of the more endearing things about this horse was his love for the harmonica. Sometimes, when time allowed, I would take a Hohner harmonica and a chair with me to the barn and sit in his stall and play a few tunes for him. He either really loved harmonica music, or he felt tremendously sorry for me. I said I played the harmonica for him, but I never said I was good at it! But he would stay in the stall the whole time I played for him (rolling his eyes at the sour notes), and that is more than I can say for most of the humans who have listened to me play.

On the good days, Pal was always there wanting and getting attention. The good days shine like newly minted gold hidden in our memory banks when we think about this special horse and his life with us.

In Search of a Cure

BEING BIG BELIEVERS IN ALTERNATIVE treatments for any disease, we never once shied away from what many would consider magical panaceas, and we didn't harbor any ill will toward traditional Western medicine and its bag of cures. We were willing to try anything to bring peace to this horse who brought so much happiness to those of us sharing life with him.

Although I will not bore you by repeating each and every downturn into the pain of a founder flare, I will tell you we tried everything new and outside the box that came along. However, there were two attempts of note that I think will interest you.

The first involved a rather severe bout that required a farm call from our trusted vet, Dr. DeAnn Hughes. At the time, we were at the end of our rope, as there had been nothing left to try since Pal's last flare. Our vet, in conjunction with Cornell University, came up with a new plan that required him to take medicine twice daily. The new thought was founder was caused by metabolic issues like Cushing's disease. Well, we bought and started administering the medicine as instructed. The whole time, Pal dutifully took whatever medicine we gave him and did so with a look of endearing trust on his face.

I have to tell you: This horse had the most expressive eyes of almost any horse I have ever been around. Watching him watch you, you saw understanding, love, mischief, happiness, disappointment, sadness, and, yes, pain. Simply observing Pal's facial expression let us know exactly and without doubt what he was thinking.

It only took one night to decide the medicine wasn't for him. He had an extremely bad reaction to it, and we found him lying in his stall the next morning, apparently close to death. His breathing was shallow, and his eyes looked as if he had been drugged with something that made him high as a kite. In other words, he looked extremely drunk. He couldn't even hold his head up, much less rise from the ground.

His reaction to the medicine called for a return trip from the vet and eventually a return to the search for a cure. Dr. Hughes gave him a shot to counteract the effects of the other medicine, and within a few hours, Pal was his old self, albeit in tremendous pain, but at least he wasn't loopy-eyed anymore.

The flare continued, and we kept searching for something to help. In the interim, we went back to the things we had been doing to help alleviate his pain until we found the next magic bullet. Fortunately, it didn't take long.

Those who have read *Unspoken Messages* know Pal has his own Facebook page called "Pal's Page," and he has developed quite a following of fans willing to put up with his goofy ways. One of them possessed the next bullet we would try.

It was in mid-May 2013 when I heard from Becky Roberts of Red Wing, Minnesota, who contacted me via Pal's Facebook page. She is a tech who works for a local veterinarian, and she had some information on an experimental drug called Laminil that was being used to treat founder/laminitis. The drug was still in the early trial phase and was not available for public use yet. Becky provided all the links and people's names we needed to see if we could get Pal in the trial. I am thankful social media has shrunk the world, making it easier to network with likeminded people. In this case, I am forever indebted to Becky for reaching out.

I spoke in depth to the two men in Colorado who were instrumental in getting the drug started in the approval process. They agreed to accept Pal in the trial even though he didn't meet all the requirements (his advanced age being a factor), and they explained the whole process to me, including instructions for the vet who would administer the drug.

I love our vet to death, but at first, she was not interested because of some negative articles she had read on medical sites. After a little begging, she agreed to administer the drug, and I stepped back and let her take over the contact with the trial administrators.

It turned out to be an extremely difficult process. First, a tourniquet is applied to the horse's leg, below the knee and above the pastern. Now, all of you horse people know you should never apply a tourniquet to a horse's leg as you can set the animal up to blow a tendon, but the process is what the process is. The tourniquet remains on the horse's leg for twenty-five minutes. To administer the medicine, a very tiny catheter has to then be threaded into a capillary just above the pastern joint. I am glad Dr. Hughes had the touch, as I couldn't see myself attempting something so delicate.

On the day of the procedure, there were several people there who were interested in seeing the procedure firsthand. Once the catheter was successfully threaded into the capillary, the medicine was trickled in over a twenty-five minute period. The left-front procedure went perfectly. During the right-front procedure, the capillary blew out halfway through the time frame. Everything about this was timed, and they couldn't stop to try to find an alternate capillary. The decision was made to allow the remaining portion of the drug to absorb through the tissue in the hopes that all of it would get where it needed to go. Sadly, things didn't work out quite as we planned.

Man plans, while God smiles.

There Is Always an Answer

F ROM THE DAY OF THE procedure until this very day, Pal has never had any more issues with his left-front hoof. For the longest time, he had no trouble with either foot. He returned to eating what all the other horses ate instead of being on a special diet. He returned to being in a pasture with other horses, eating grass, and simply being a horse. He returned to being ridden on a regular basis—his ultimate joy.

The vet came by a few weeks after the procedure, and I turned Pal loose in the arena area and let him put on a show for her. She couldn't believe the improvement in Pal, and she paid him the highest compliment he could possibly get; she said if he wasn't cured, he was as close as any horse she had ever seen. She now believed Laminil worked.

We had talked about redoing his right front and even got as far as trying to get another dose of Laminil. However, even though the trial phase was complete, the drug still had not been approved for use in horses. In other words, until the drug was approved for use, we could not get anymore. Dang it. The trial was over in 2013, but Laminil was not approved for use in treating laminitis until 2016.

Since the problems with the right front continued, it was time to start searching for a cure once again. This time, we were under the gun and watching the clock. Changes were coming to our lives—major changes that would affect every single being at the stables. Some of the changes would be heartbreaking and require a ton of process time. But first ...

The Search Concludes

Since publishing the book *Unspoken Messages*, I have been fortunate to meet many people across this country and, indeed, the world. One of those at the top of the list is Kim Thomas of Texas who owns and operates a large horse rescue in Bartonville and Pilot Point, just south of Dallas. Through her work, she is in contact with many wonderful farriers and other horse health experts.

It was through her that we met some other people who have had success in treating founder. We had Pal x-rayed yet again and sent the most recent film to a group in Texas who specializes in corrective trimming and shoeing. Now, I must say, I have never been a proponent of shoeing, but we were running out of ways to help Pal. The group studied the film and made their suggestions.

They recommended Pal be trimmed with a roll-over break to the front of the hoof and the rest of the foot trimmed to offset the rotation of the coffin bone. This was a unique way of looking at things. If you can't change the rotation, change the foot to offset it. After trimming, a shoe would be formed to fit the trim for stability and comfort. Also, there was a new product on the market. It was made up of two different caulk-like substances that are applied to the sole and frog area of the hoof and allowed to harden, which happens rather quickly. After they dry, it creates a gel-like pad that supports the sole plate of the foot. All this sounded to me like it might work, so I made arraignments for the group to meet with my farrier and explain what they wanted him to do.

Joe Dirolf, our farrier, arrived early one spring morning to try the latest magic and see what our results would be. Well, apparently Pal had never been shod before. I could tell he was a bit antsy, but he stood fairly well for the long procedure. After everything was trimmed and applied, I led Pal out of the barn breezeway, and I swear he moved like a new horse. He was able to turn around in the breezeway of the barn instead of being led outside to make a large loop. He also backed the eighty-foot length of the barn breezeway without any issues at all. Backing up is extremely hard on a foundered horse, and it is usually difficult to get them to do it successfully.

The instructions indicated Pal needed to be reset and trimmed every six weeks; in addition, he was to have the gel pad reapplied at each trimming. Now all that remained was to watch him and see how he moved about. We watched him closely for the next six weeks.

He had become a new horse. He became the horse we knew he could become all along. To watch him move, you would never suspect he was a severely foundered horse. We would put him in the arena by himself, and he would run, buck, and fart like crazy. People were riding him again. Pal became what he always wanted to be—just another horse (albeit a famous one) at the stables. As I looked back down the very long road we had traveled together, I knew we had reached a point where this foundered horse could once again just be himself—without pain. The ultimate goal had been achieved! The timing of this success was important, as things at the stables were changing rapidly.

The Constant Is Change

I N THE BOOK *UNSPOKEN MESSAGES,* I wrote, "We all reach a point in life where we must realize that forward is the only direction, now is the only time, and change is the only constant." When I wrote those words, I had no idea how prophetic they would become in this life of mine, and I had no idea how much the coming change would cause me to feel such a range of emotions. Those emotions traveled from complete, overwhelming sadness to the contented happiness that came with knowing I made the best and only decision I could ever imagine with the circumstances given.

See, when we rolled the dice on this latest treatment for Pal, we knew our time together was going to end much quicker than we envisioned. A parting was on the horizon and had to come quickly—or quickly as time relates to the fixed speed in which we all exist. It is a bit odd, but we all experience the slowing and speeding of time, even though it never really changes; it only seems to.

My wife Jennifer's parents had been on a slow decline, and if we live long enough, we'll all experience the same slowing as age catches up with us. We had watched this decline, sometimes from a distance and sometimes up close and personal. For a while, it was not something we talked about much, but you can only ignore the buffalo in the barn lot for so long before you have to do something with it.

Jennifer is from Maine, and that is where her parents, Bob and Arlene, lived and wanted to die when the time came. They would not move to Kentucky and let us help with their care, and I do not blame them. Happiness and quality of life are paramount in writing the last chapter of this life's book. So we needed to go to them. The decision to sell the farm and stables was a difficult one to make after almost twenty years of successfully creating a peaceful place for horses and humans alike. Boarders become family, and we were surrounded by great friends. There was much to do before closing the door for the last time. We had to learn to dance with a broken heart and seek happiness and direction once again as we moved forward.

Not only did we have to find a buyer for the farm but, hopefully, the stables as a business so the boarders could remain behind us, enjoying the haven we had created for them. We started marketing our home in October 2015 without much initial luck in a depressed economy. The decision to close the business and sell the inventory separately from the land and buildings was made. The farm sold a week later, and we got busy liquidating the rest of our life and seeking a new one.

We also had three horses to consider, and they were all an equal part of the family, with none more important than the other. I never imagined a future that didn't include the three of them. Emotions cycled back and forth from tears to elation. We had Pal (of course); Bo, Jennifer's personal horse (and the youngster of the group); and Annie, our long-term, do-everything horse and also the one with the most seniority.

I mentioned Kim Thomas earlier in the story. She and her husband, Brad, live in Texas. I met the family approximately four years ago when I traveled to Texas for a fundraising event at Ranch Hand Rescue and a book signing. We became fast and, to this day, best friends. It is a good thing they live in Texas, as I do not think any other state could hold her big heart. I have lost track of the number of horses Kim has rescued and taken care of.

Kim is lucky to have a great foreman named Pedro who works with her, helping with the care of horses that were given up on by others. He does most of the hands-on work with the horses that come in from all over America. Pedro trains horses, breaks them to ride, and sees to their daily care. He is an all-around great guy with a quick smile and an abundance of knowledge about our equine companions. In addition, numerous people also volunteer their time to help care for these abused, abandoned, and neglected horses.

Kim agreed to take Pal and Annie. Both of these well-loved horses had a lot of history behind them, and both came with their unique and complicated medical issues. Neither would have adjusted to the brutal winters in the northeast; they would fare much better in the Texas climate. Bo would travel to Maine with us along with three rescue cats and a rescue dog. I felt we needed some seeds from Kentucky to make a new home our home. The heaviest decisions made, we waited for everything to come together, all the time dreading the day two of our beloved family members would board a trailer and leave us for the last time.

It is said that moving is one of the most stressful things you can experience, especially cross-country moving. I can certainly attest to the truthfulness of that statement because everyone was completely strained to the max. The farm, land, and buildings had sold, and the inventory was rapidly leaving the farm. The boarders all left, having found new homes for their charges.

During the inventory sale, our days would start at five o'clock in the morning and generally wouldn't end until after nine o'clock at night. The business of dealing with other people occupied our minds and bodies to the point where thoughts of transporting the horses had taken on more of an afterthought status. They were never out of our minds but were far enough back to allow us to manage the sale.

> Change is the ever-present center.
> Be willing to give up what you
> are in return
> for what you could be.

Loaded Up and Headed West

WE SOLD THE FARM TO the Razon family. With Ryan Razon retiring from the army after years of traveling the world, he and his wife, Elli, and their two children, Kai and Rylee, planned to make Kentucky their forever home. We became fast friends in a short period of time and couldn't have left the place in better hands. They are raising goats, and we love seeing the videos of the newborns playing and having fun.

As happy as we were to have sold the home place to people who would love and care for it as we did, we now had to deal with the negative part of the equation and send a couple of horses who had been a part of our family for years to a new forever home. We knew Pal and Annie were headed to Kim's place in Texas; it was only a matter of lining up transportation. As easy as it may seem when viewing it logically, it becomes much more difficult when emotional attachment is involved.

How does one part company willingly with animals that have asked nothing more than to have your company in their lives? We are stewards of many animals, and they are loved and cared for equally. It is almost like having a bunch of kids. We love them equally but for different reasons, as they each bring something unique to our lives.

I carry many wonderful memories of each of them and always will. There had been many days over the years when I had spent the night in the barn with a sick or needy horse. When Pal would be experiencing a severe flare, we would sometimes sit on the stall floor and hold his head as he cycled in and out of pain. Never once was there a sign he wanted to give up and get the inevitable over with—not one single time. He did, however, find comfort in our presence, calmness in our spoken words, and peace in the warmth of our touch. As long as being there brought healing to him, then we would be right there beside him.

And then there was Annie, the does-it-all horse and the first one I bought when I started the stables. My most fond memories of her include the numerous times she would actually wake me up when she was about to deliver a foal. I would sleep on hay bales in the breezeway of the barn on the nights I thought she would foal. I was always sleeping on the other side of her stall wall, and she could hang her head over the wall and shake me. Sometimes when I was sleeping heavily she would have to shake me harder, and she wasn't shy about letting me know the show was about to start. Annie always wanted company when giving birth. I have so many memories, so many smiles, so much laughter, and so much fun, and all of it would now be balanced by heartache.

Oh, trust me, there were also moments of frustration. For instance, Pal, in all the years he was there, had never been shod. We preferred to keep our horses barefoot unless we had a good reason to shoe them. As I wrote earlier in this story, a form of shoeing that was performed on him was working wonderfully, and it was about time to reset him for the trip to Texas. Little did either Joe the farrier or I know how much Pal hated the process, especially after he had tolerated it fairly well the first time. On the day Pal had to be reset, he threw an absolute fit, almost to the point of hurting Joe. Never in all the years Pal was with us did he ever act out toward anyone, but it was apparent he really disliked what was going on.

I found myself wishing I had trained him for the process so it wouldn't be such a big deal to him. I tried several things to calm him down, but nothing worked until I had to employ a twitch. For the uninitiated, a twitch is something you tightened up around a portion of the horse's nose. It is relatively painless but is reported to release endorphins in horses and give them a sense of calmness and something else to think about while being worked on. It worked but not as well as I have seen it work on other horses. He still managed to throw enough of a fit to scare the two of us a bit. He squealed, pawed, and carried on as if we were torturing him instead of helping him to walk pain-free. Naturally, he could not differentiate between the two. Eventually, the deed was done, but Pal didn't forget what I had done to him. Oh, he came around, but he didn't come around quickly. He shunned me for about three weeks. He wouldn't even look at me when I called, and if I walked in the lot where he was, he would walk away without as much as a glance.

I guess the most surprising thing was the humanlike reaction from Pal. The looks of anger, disbelief, and disappointment were as evident on his face as they would be on a human counterpart who felt slighted by some action. His displeasure with me lasted almost until the day he left for Texas. It was a sad time at the stables and not the way I wanted things to end after all the good years we'd had together. Sadly, the disappointment with me was replaced with looks of uncertainty and fear that showed plainly in his eyes the day he and Annie loaded on the trailer to leave their longtime home. Our hearts were breaking because both of them had the same look, a look that said they were being abandoned. There are those among you who might say my guilt played into my interpretation of his facial expression, but I know what I saw, and I wasn't alone. Horses have been treated as livestock for so long that people fail to really see the depth of their souls and their wisdom. I am glad I, and those around me, can really see what is going on in a horse's mind even though it hurts to know sometimes.

I guess one of the hardest things I have ever done was to load those horses on a trailer, knowing the whole time it could be the last time I would see them. The looks they gave Jennifer and me had both of us in tears. We both spent a lot of time talking to Pal and Annie, trying to reassure them everything would be okay and we would see them again. As the truck pulled out of the barn drive, Pal could be seen looking behind him from the trailer, making eye contact with me and gazing at his home for the last time, wondering what was happening in his life. A thought entered my mind, and I wondered if he thought we were getting rid of him because of the way he had been acting since farrier day. I prayed that was not the case. This horse had to realize how much we loved him and how much we hated sending him off to another place.

And … if you think I cared less for Annie because she wasn't mentioned as much as Pal, it is not true. Annie was the first horse I bought when I retired and started my business. She was a lesson horse, a partner on a rough day, and a trusted trail horse. She taught Boy Scouts the horsemanship merit badge classes, had babies, gave rides to the elderly, and kept all the other horses in line. There was never a doubt who the herd boss was. Annie went about life maintaining a very stoic demeanor. Everything was just another day. Although she loaded with a look that seemed to beg an answer to the question, "Where are you sending me?" she loaded well and did as I asked. That was the way Annie did things. Sadly, this would be the last time I would ever see this horse who was such a calming presence on the farm. She left me with a trunk full of memories, a belly full of laughs, and a mind full of lessons she taught. I can only hope I made her proud by learning what she taught. I also hope she left knowing we counted her as family and she was loved unconditionally.

One of the many pluses of living in this world shrunken by so many means of instant communication is we are blessed to meet many people life would have kept from us if not for the internet. One of those virtual friends is Gayle. Some time ago, she forwarded me a poem her father,

Leslie, wrote about selling his farm and moving to town. I am grateful Gayle and her three sisters allowed me to share the poem with you. It sure touched my heart, and I realized I was feeling the same thing about selling and moving.

Movin' to Town Today

Takin' a last look at the old place today,
Never did get that fence on the north side to stay.
Movin' to town today

I kinda thought I'd finally get
That old barn painted someday,
I guess someone else will anyway.
Movin' to town today

Well the stall walls look sturdy and clean,
Those walls have held the good and the mean.
Movin' to town today

I can look out at my sandy arena
And remember the very spot,
Where I stepped up on that dun
And wished I had not.
Movin' to town today

The yard looks ok to a wrangler like me,
I'll do better with the yard in town, wait and see.
Movin' to town today

Leslie Wayne Jones
July 11, 1936–August 5, 2000

The Connection Is Forever

WHEN PAL AND ANNIE LOADED on the trailer for the trip to Texas, I promised them both this wouldn't be the last they would see of me. As much as I pride myself on my ability to keep promises, one of these promises would not be kept. About a month after arriving at their new home, Miss Annie passed away. As sad as it was, she was blessed by not being alone and in fear as the inevitable for us all claimed her early one morning. Pedro, the do-everything cowboy for the rescue farm, and Kim were present when Annie peacefully crossed over. She was held, petted, and cooed to as she spotted and sped over the bridge, tail high, whinnies ringing over the hills and through the valleys so all present across the bridge could hear her happiness and know she had arrived.

Here on Earth, we felt her passing as a gentle warm breeze on an otherwise cold winter's day. She had safely arrived in the after. Once she arrived, she remembered this place from before and knew she was here for a rest before continuing the never-ending cycle. Once again, all was right in the world and things made sense.

Every animal domesticated by humans
deserves to be provided with
care and treated with compassion.

Peace through Magic

THOSE OF YOU WHO KNOW me or those who have read the book *Unspoken Messages* are aware I live with a cancer diagnosis. In 2008 I was diagnosed with a rare blood cancer related to two tours in Vietnam. Initially, I was given an unsolicited prognosis of living three more years at the most. Well, it is almost twelve years later, and I am still going strong.

Without going into too many details that are covered in the other book, let's just say I embraced many alternative beliefs and alternative medicines. By embrace, I mean I totally believe in things many of you might not consider, and the things I believe in work wonderfully for me because of those beliefs.

Through the power of my book and during my travels since my diagnosis, I have been blessed to have met many people in the alternative belief/treatment world. They brought unbelievable magic to my life and challenged every belief I have been spoon-fed my whole life. They opened my eyes to other possibilities, and there are always other possibilities.

One of the most talented people I have ever met is Holly Tagg of Minneapolis, Minnesota. Holly is a psychic and animal communicator and operates her business, which is called Solomon's Ring-Holly Tagg Psychic/Animal Communicator. I have used her talents several times to get insight into the actions of animals and have always been given logical, easy-to-understand messages from the minds of animals.

I contacted Holly about Pal and Annie, as I needed to know what they were thinking and feeling the day they left. The looks on their faces had left me with a heart full of pain and feelings of guilt, and I was seeking clarity and peace with my decisions.

The Silent Conversation

HOLLY SENT ME THE FOLLOWING after her conversations with Pal and Annie:

> Animals aren't normally chatty. They are happy to answer questions but don't usually go on and on. Pal is definitely an exception, though, and once started, had a lot to share. He is a beautiful being!
>
> The first thing Pal told me was to tell you he is sorry. It was just too hard to say goodbye. He knows it was hard for you too. He thought if he wasn't being his usual good self, maybe you wouldn't love him as much and it would make things easier. Pal said he knew in reality that wasn't the truth—deep love never dies—but it was the only thing he could come up with at the time.
>
> Pal says on some level he knew all along that you wouldn't always be together. He really cherishes his time with you and felt you both had so much to teach each other.
>
> He said you both taught each other about love and determination, and you helped each other heal. He says he helped you to shift your focus and within that, you learned a lot about life and overcoming obstacles. He says your faith in him taught him he had the power to allow himself to heal.

He is telling me all your help enabled him to succeed in healing, and his success is helping other horses heal that may not have made it otherwise. He says the extra care and out-of-the-box thinking has proven to others that this horrible disease can be healed. That the standard protocol isn't all there is and answers do exist.

He says just as you overcame the impossible, so did he with your love and support. He thanks you for that from the bottom of his heart.

He told me you saved him and many others, and as he is telling me this he fills me with a profound feeling of love. He says you gave him a voice. You gave him a chance and you understood him for the being he is. He said he did the same for you and loved every minute of it.

He is telling me that through you telling his story and believing in him, he has been able to touch so many. He ponders a bit and says, "You know, some may find it funny that a horse cares about touching and moving people." What is it that makes us reach beyond our boundaries, and embrace other beings who are so different and yet so similar? Why are we not content to stay in our own worlds and interact with those who are so much like us in body and mind? He says for him it is about love. It is about compassion. It is about curiosity. It is about lifting others up. He says it lights him up inside to see the smile on someone's face when they see him. The excitement they get when they spend time with him. Most of all he likes how peaceful people become. They tell you their secrets; they allow you into a part of them very few get to see. He says he has heard many secrets and soothed many a soul, and that is a life well lived. You helped him do that, and he helped you do the same. You can't do any better than that.

He wants you to know although it isn't quite the same as being together in person, you can talk to him any time. He will always be there for you.

What an amazing being! I loved every minute of my time with Pal!

Holly asked Annie how she felt about leaving for Texas.

She says it was sad; goodbyes always are. She said she completely understood everyone's reasoning, and it all made sense, so she was okay with it. She is telling me you did much research and soul-searching to come to this decision. She really appreciates all the care and thoughtfulness you put into choosing the perfect location so she and Pal could be happy and loved. Annie has a very matriarchal energy about her. She is a caretaker and she always loved her role, watching over everyone.

Annie was just as Holly described her. She was our do-everything horse, and she did everything asked of her well. She was a mother and teacher to the young horses and was without any doubt from other horses the alpha mare of the stables.

Holly continued:

She is also telling me she had a sense she wouldn't be around much longer. She said she didn't know for sure, but in her gut she knew it was important to accompany Pal. She knew he needed a friend. Pal needed someone to help him walk through all his new endeavors. She would be someone to remind him of home and be a comfort until he got his feet under him in the new place. She knew he was happy and in good hands when she left and that is what freed her up to go. She felt accomplished, grateful, and happy with all she had done in her life. She has such wonderful memories of her home and family in Kentucky.

Holly's gifts, talent, ability, compassion, and strength of character brought me peace. It let me know my decisions were sound, and no matter the pain of longing, we would all adapt to the new normal. As I said earlier, "We all reach a point in life where we must realize that forward is the only direction, now is the only time, and change is the only constant."

My life is blessed with many good and talented friends. I am thankful Holly has such a gift and is willing to share it with others. My heart is beginning to heal, and its scars will make me even stronger in the days to come.

Answers are found in silence and solitude.

From the Mind of the Horse:
Laying the Ground Rules

I T HAS LONG BEEN MY contention that horses are old souls with much magic about them and the ability to teach and touch those who are open to the grays that live within the black-and-white lives we often lead. It is one thing to have such a belief and quite another to try to convince others of the possibilities that live in those gray areas of existence. This story is one of those attempts, so keep turning the pages and don't plan anything too ambitious for a little while. You might just walk away with a glimpse through the veil.

We all age as we walk through this journey called life, and while traveling, we accumulate lessons that are stored in the form of memories. All those lessons teach, and each lesson stays with us in our bank of memories. Some of those memories, like of the death of a loved animal, will start out as sad or hurtful only to change with time to memories we treasure more than any riches we have stored in our lives' trunks. The pain of longing inevitably fades, leaving the moments that really mattered in their wake. If you are lucky, and I think most of you will be, time will prove the most valuable gifts we have are the memories we make. I also believe there is more to this life than we have been led to believe ... Magic and possibilities exist.

Unfortunately, some of these memories may carry a heavy load of guilt. Carried too far, longtime guilt will inevitably result in disease or at least a poor quality of life. Let me show you how to get rid of some of that guilt. Forgive yourself and move on without the weight of guilt wrapped around your neck. Learn that magical possibilities exist and life holds more of this magic than we ever thought possible.

Drawing on my experience from things I did earlier in this life of mine, let's do a little investigation. Let's look into the ability of horses to remember you even after long periods of time. Do they react when they see you after a long hiatus? Did you possibly sell or trade them and then see them at a later date? Did life get so busy that you haven't been able to spend much time with them? Let's move on and discover the depth of this soul possessed by the horse. I'll bet some of you will be in for a surprise.

Trust me when I say that there is
more to this life than you
have been led to believe.
Magic and possibilities exist.

Remembering a Bucket List Dream

THE YEAR WAS 1971, AND I was returning from Vietnam for the second time. The difference this time was I had completed my active duty obligation to the US Army. I was a free man! Oh, I still had a reserve status to serve, but the chances of being called back were somewhere between zero and less than zero. I had long planned to return home via train, as I had a burning desire to see this country the way my forefathers saw it. At the time, we still had a train depot in Elizabethtown, my childhood home, so travel would practically be door to door.

Fate would intervene, and that intervention would last for more than forty years. I was sent home from Vietnam a week early because my father was scheduled to have an experimental surgery to replace the arteries in his legs. Even though they said there was a good chance he would not make it through the surgery, he surprised all of them with his hard headedness and not only recovered but lived another seven years afterward. Due to the circumstances, I rushed home by plane and put the train travel on the back burner.

Fast-forward to the year 2017 when I was planning a return trip to Texas to see my friends Kim and Brad Thomas who run a huge horse rescue. They take care of dozens of horses that have been abandoned, abused, neglected, or were simply due to be sold for meat in other countries. They also take care of the famous Pal, a horse I have written about many times. The reason for the trip was to reconnect with Pal and see if, after two years, he would remember me. While in the planning stages, I had the idea to check off a major entry on my bucket list. I would make this trip via rail.

Packing proof that dreams come true if you keep them close, I boarded my first train on October 27, 2017. It was with a childlike grin on my face that I set about unpacking in my sleeper car and then sat down and awaited the magic. From the very first push of movement, the first gentle roll of the car, the first clickety-clack of the wheels rolling over seams and junctions, I fell deeply in love with this old method of travel and plan on many return trips.

Since arriving at a place of peace several years ago, I normally sleep the night through without interruption. However, I still enjoy those unscheduled wake-ups in the middle of the night. You know the ones where you go to a window and simply look at the world. You never know what you might see or experience under the spell of four-o'clock darkness. I was blessed to awake at four o'clock in the morning during the first night of travel. I opened the curtains and witnessed magic. Outside, heavy fog enshrouded the trees in a ghostly coat of white, leaving the skeletal, leafless branches reaching through the mist in either a peaceful embrace or a quiet warning of coming horror, with only your imagination free to decide which belief to own. Unsure yet of which, I lay mesmerized by and reflecting on the scene before me. Sleep called for me once again, and I closed the curtain and returned to bed to slowly drift away after covering myself with a blanket of peace and eschewing any fear from the vision. I was comfortable with my choice and soundly slept the rest of the night away. After a two-day trip, I arrived in Dallas, Texas, with a good case of vertigo but still packing the childlike glee I had started with.

Only the person who is willing to take risk
is free.
From risk, comes growth.

A Long Overdue Reunion

I ADMIT I HAD SOME TREPIDATION about my coming reunion with Pal. After all, he had been in Texas for almost two years and was by all reports comfortable with his new home and standing. You see, Pal has the run of the ranch. He has his own big stall to stay in at night or during inclement weather. Each morning he is simply let out to go wherever he desires. He has his herd of friends, and he has standing within that herd. He also has unlimited access to the hay storage. The boy never goes hungry. My worries were twofold: one, would he even remember me, and two, would he see me as someone who was coming to take him back to Kentucky?

Here I was in Texas, wondering if Pal would remember me and how he might react. Would he simply not pay me any more attention than anyone else there? Would he be angry, disappointed, sad, questioning, or any of the other negative emotions that seem to show themselves during times like these? Or would he be his regular, kind, and understanding self as described by psychic and animal communicator Holly Tagg? Isn't it funny how we humans seem to gravitate toward the negative when faced with the unknown?

It was a bright, sunshiny, Texas kind of day where sunglasses were a requirement and jackets were optional. Kim did the driving, and we lapsed into a comfortable silence during the ride to the Pilot Point ranch. My thoughts were on the constant, nagging worry this might not go as I wished.

Kim and Brad Thomas have become my close friends. Their hearts and mine share this love of animals in general but for horses specifically. It is like we have been part of this journey together forever. I have always loved the Pilot Point location. As you pull in through the electric gate, you are seemingly and suddenly transported to a Lexington, Kentucky, horse farm. You are surrounded by white fences, barns, paddocks, and, most of all, horses and more horses. At the time, there were more than fifty-five horses at this particular location, and all of them were rescues that had been given a slice of heaven in which to spend the rest of their years. They came from abusive owners. They came from neglect, abandonment, kill pens (for those uninitiated, kill pens are where horses are sold for slaughter and human consumption overseas), over breeding, and other situations that reflect quite negatively on the human race as it relates to our collective treatment of animals that ask nothing in return but our company. As sad as the situation is, there are angels on Earth like Kim and all those who help her care for these animals. They started the Thomas Foundation Second Chance Rescue, a 501(c)(3) nonprofit agency that offers lifetime care for those unadoptable horses and a foot up to others that can be adopted to good homes. No one puts more love into horses than they do at Pilot Point, and I was thrilled when Kim agreed to take Pal into the fold. In addition to the Pilot Point location, they have another forty horses at other locations around the Bartonville/ Pilot Point area.

As we pulled in through the gate, I felt home again. I have a few places in the world that affect me this way, and I am lucky to visit all of them with regularity. The plan was this: Pal would be out and about, doing what he normally does. I would enter the barn where he could not see me but would be able to hear what I was about to do. I would play the harmonica for him like I used to in Kentucky when he was under the weather. Then, all we could do is wait to see his reaction. Would he remember? Would he run toward me or gallop away? It was time to quit worrying and play. So I took out my harmonica and started playing "My Old Kentucky Home." I was rusty but soon fell into the rhythm.

The response was a bit delayed, but oh, what a response it was! As Pedro (the number-one ranch hand and trainer) said, "That is the fastest I have seen him run since he got here." Foundered horses don't generally run anywhere, but Pal motored pretty fast, straight up to the barn and straight beside me, rubbing against my side as he went past. It was like my soul cried tears of happiness as I watched this old horse come to me from across the pasture at a sustained trot. A huge grin spread all the way across my face. I felt humbled in his presence yet validated in my thoughts that horses do remember and remember well.

Shortly after Pal arrived in the barn, he became distant. I feared this could happen, and Kim and I had talked about it. I let him have his space and simply watched his actions. He had a question; I could tell, but interpreting his question would take a little thought and guidance from the powers of the universe. For the rest of this first day, I let Pal go about his way and watched as he interacted with other people and horses. Obviously, he was a very happy horse, living in a caring and loving environment.

The next day, I caught up with Pal behind the hay barn. I brought a halter, lead line, and a few grooming supplies with me. I didn't bring any scissors, as I had been banned from cutting Pal's mane after a disastrous maiden attempt at giving him a trim. My wife and Pal's fans on Facebook were ready to string me up. At the time, I thought he was pretty cute, but I'm fairly certain I was the only one.

Pal and I had a long talk while I groomed him, and he seemed completely caught up in the cadence and rhythm of my voice. I spoke in plain English, just exactly the way I would talk to a human. I told him with words and the accompanying emotions that I was not there to take him back to Kentucky. I could see how happy he was and how many friends surrounded him. I could see how important the daily interaction with other horses and farm animals was to him, and I would never take him away from what made him happy. It is up to you to judge whether he understood my words and emotions, but I know what I believe. After the talk and for the remaining days at the ranch, Pal stayed by my side. And the final day as I was about to leave, he curled his head and neck around my shoulders and pulled me in for a horse hug.

My heart is at peace. I know Pal is where he is supposed to be, doing what he is supposed to do. He is the greeter of the ranch, the first one to gravitate toward visitors, especially children. He seems a king, and Pilot Point his kingdom.

The universe once again worked its magic. It led me to write a book, which led to many friendships across the world. It led me to a little corner of Texas, a place where I was comfortable being surrounded by those who believe as I do—animals are old souls with much to teach. All we have to do is be open to the magic. Pal is home for the rest of this life, whether it is another week or many years. The king is holding court ... daily.

Peace awaits at the end of a well-traveled journey.

I have interviewed many people who shared accounts of animals remembering them after extended periods of time apart. This story comes from Kathy Smith who, along with her husband, owns Maine Horse and Rider, an upscale tack store in Holden, Maine. She was the owner of a Lipizzaner-Thoroughbred cross that she traded for the day he was born.

Regal and Kathy

KATHY SAID, "WE USED TO have a small saw mill in a little town in northern Maine, and I took lessons at a local dressage barn that also bred a lot of horses. We traded sawdust for lessons and ended up trading lumber for Regal, a Lipizzaner-Thoroughbred foal. I was there just hours after he was born and saw him almost every day. After two years, we ended up moving a couple of hours away, and not being able to find affordable board, I left him at the dressage barn. Regal wasn't going to start his training for another year or so. The barn owner really wanted to buy him back, so after another year, I finally sold him back to her. We had two young girls at that point and had just bought and begun renovating an 1850s farmhouse, so there was no time for a young horse."

Kathy hadn't been back for nearly two years when she decided to take her girls up one afternoon. The owner had a huge pasture at the top of the hill behind the barn where the younger ones stayed. Her before horse was in a group of about fifteen to twenty horses that were way up the hill under a tree. Not being comfortable taking her two young girls into such a large pasture with young yahoos, she called Regal like she used to when he was little. "How's my boy?" she would call in a high voice, and she would make the word *boy* sound like a bit of a nicker. The minute he heard her, his head whipped up, and he looked over.

She called again, and he bolted from the herd and galloped all the way down to them! Kathy couldn't believe his reaction; of course, she was just overwhelmed that he remembered and cared enough about her to run down to her when he heard her voice. It was such a heartwarming feeling to know she had had such a good impact on a horse.

They patted and rubbed him over the fence, scratched him in all his favorite places, and then, leaning in over the electric wire for one more pat, she accidentally touched the hot wire. There was a Swiss army knife in her front pocket. It hit the wire and sent a horrendous shock through her feet, up through her right arm, and right into poor Regal's face. He leaped back, almost sitting down and then whirled away. Kathy felt so bad. He wouldn't come back down again that day no matter how many times she called.

> Life is a school where you learn to
> remember what you already know.

I have been lucky while researching this book to meet and talk to people from all over the United States and beyond about their experiences with horses. Although all of us are different in our own ways, our experiences with animals are the same, just in different locations. Teresa Cory from Indiana shared her story about a reunion with her horse Cherokee.

Remembering Teresa

TERESA NO LONGER RODE BECAUSE of serious injuries received in an earlier horseback riding accident in which her pelvis was fractured. Her longtime horse Cherokee was not the one she was riding when the accident occurred, but she knew he would be better off with a new keeper instead of being a pasture pet. With a breaking heart, she sold him to a friend. Teresa got caught up in life for a while, and thoughts of Cherokee had to take a back seat to Teresa's sister who was dying of cystic fibrosis. It was sometime after things settled down that Teresa decided to go visit Cherokee and wondered if he would remember her.

I will let her tell this part of the story:

> I changed my clothes and decided I would go see Cherokee and make sure he was good. When I was driving up to my friend's place, that horse heard my truck coming, and I could see him running toward the house. I pulled in and got out and was heading toward the fence. I could hear him whinnying all the way. He was the only horse running to me. By this time, I was crying and sliding under the fence. He came to me, and I wrapped my arms around his neck. He dropped his head over my shoulder and was nuzzling me and softly

nickering. We stood embracing for a long while as I
cried and told him I loved him so.

Teresa still visits Cherokee, and yes, he remembers her each time.

Once made, the connection is forever.

On the subject of connections, I have a little aside of my own to add to the mix. It took place in October 2017 while I was in Texas visiting my good friends Kim and Brad Thomas.

The Many Lives of Dakota

IT WAS ONE OF THOSE perfect Texas fall days. Bright sunshine from a surreal, clear-blue sky warmed the skin where it kissed it, but the breeze held a promise of cooler things to come. We were at Thor and Athena's Promise Sanctuary located in Argyle, Texas. The sanctuary, a 501(c)(3) nonprofit, is owned by Lynn and Paul Cairney. They give horseback riding lessons and rescue draft horses. Once a year, they have an open house and invite their friends and children who take lessons there to attend a theme party called Boo at the Barn. Attendees and horses alike dress in costumes to fit the theme. I met bat-horses, kings and queens, and several more costume-dressed horses and humans. They even had a potbellied pig in a wheelbarrow. During the open house, attendees and their horses also participated in Nicker Treat where horses and humans alike get treats. It was a fun day, filled with horse people and animal lovers.

They set up different stations with activities for the horses and people, like bobbing for apples for the horses, which was a laughter-inducing event to watch. I was amazed at the amount of try in some horses. They also had an obstacle course for the riders to navigate, not to mention enough food to feed a small army. It was a grand day, and I was blessed to meet a ton of like-minded people who strongly believe in the ethical and humane treatment of animals. It is as if we have a creed we stick to in which animals domesticated by man are due kindness, compassion, and care, not abuse, neglect, and abandonment. After all, these animals ask nothing of us but our company and care. In return, they show us the magic of the universe.

It was during this open house that I met—or should I say reconnected with—a horse I apparently knew before. I say apparently, but in the end, you will be the judge.

I was sitting on a blanket-covered straw bale watching the festivities when a young lady led a roan-looking Appaloosa past me. While walking past, the horse actually did a double take when it saw me. You have had people look at you when they think they know you or you are familiar to them. Well, that is exactly what happened here. After the double take, the horse kept its eyes, or at least one of them, on me the whole time it was being led past. Her eyes seemed to implore me to remember her like she did me. It was the oddest sensation, and one I have never had before. I ended up entranced by this horse and continued to watch her while she was in the arena area. As I watched her, she was just as intent upon watching me. Each time I took my eyes off her to look at some other attention-grabbing event and then looked back, she was still watching me. After a bit of this visual inquiry, I went into the arena and asked the owner, Lacey Atkinson, about the history of the horse. She had owned the horse since she was rescued at the age of ten months, and she was now ten years old. Her name was Dakota, and she had been neglected and was in pretty bad shape when rescued but had since been returned to health and happiness.

After studying Dakota's past, I came to the conclusion there was zero possibility our paths had crossed prior to that day. How was it possible for her to look at me as if she knew me and was imploring me with her eyes to remember our history? Was she a ghost from my past coming to the forefront of my thoughts via some long-harbored guilt? As a firm and fervent believer in reincarnation, does the same thing happen to the soul energy of animals? Are their souls immortal like ours? Did this horse possess the soul of some long-departed horse from my life? I know what my soul is telling me. It says I do, in fact, know Dakota; I am just unable to place her. She is some part of my past and will be some part of my future. I see life as a constant cycle of learning and experiencing. Animals are no different than us in the soul department and far better than us in the level of their enlightenment.

As I continued to watch the horse, Lacey began to lead her out. I nudged Kim, who was sitting beside me and said, "Watch what this horse is doing." As Dakota was led past me, she not only watched me but turned her head as she walked in order to hold the eye contact. I am grateful nothing was in her way because she would not break eye contact. Kim was awed, and I felt validated in my belief that horses are old souls with much to teach.

Interpretation is up to us, and the first step to interpretation is to open ourselves to the magical possibilities that exist all around us. Instead of merely looking, we need to actually see. We need to be willing to believe things could be much different than the set of ideals and beliefs we have spent our lives believing to be absolute truth. Don't wait for some life-challenging event to happen to you before you are willing to see the amazing things that surround us daily.

I am not one to believe in coincidence at all.
There is a purpose to this life. Plant
seeds of kindness, be caring to others,
show compassion, and be at peace. Once mastered, watch
your purpose become clear.

This story about remembering comes from an experience Sarah Gordon had with her horse Mickey Blue. Sarah relayed her story to me about their reunion after many years apart.

Remembering Sarah

Around August 2010, Sarah purchased her first horse. She had been working with horses for years and had been dreaming of this day for even longer. She had finally saved enough money to buy her first horse. A friend of hers heard she was searching and told her about a beautiful 2004 paint stallion for sale but only green broke. She drove two hours to see him and excitedly walked out to the barn and runs where the owner stated he would be. And there he was ... He was pretty well covered in muck and mud; she could hardly see his coloring and markings other than his facial markings and one soul-piercing blue eye. Sarah said, "I loved him already." She climbed through the paneling into his muck run for a closer look at him, not caring about the owner's warnings regarding his behavior. He walked right up to her and ever so gently placed his forehead directly into her chest and closed his eyes. She immediately said, "I will take him."

Sarah brought Mickey Blue home to the farm where she worked, and they built a bond from there. They were inseparable until she had to give him away to a friend she worked with at the horse farm due to home issues. She was devastated and felt as though she was abandoning him. She heavily felt the emotions of being crushed, heartbroken, and ashamed. The lady Sarah had sold him to wound up selling him, and over the next seven years, he was sold five times. Sarah felt terrible, and over the course of those seven years, she tried to buy him back multiple times. She missed him dearly and constantly thought of him. She cried for him often, and then it happened.

It was August 21, 2017, and Sarah had been having a very rough day. She was sitting on the porch with her friend (the one she originally gave the horse to all those years ago) when she found out her friend had bought Mickey Blue back for Sarah. She bought him back for her and had planned to try to surprise her but couldn't hold it in. Sarah had never cried so hard out of pure happiness; it was overwhelming! The next day they trailered out to pick him up, and on the way, Sarah couldn't help but wonder … Would he remember her? Would he be upset with her? She had so many questions and so many emotions that she found herself fighting hard to control them.

After their arrival, she had to walk all the way out into the pasture to fetch him. He didn't realize who she was until he lowered his head and looked at her in the eye. He sniffed her hands and up her arm to her hair and then placed his muzzle right on her mouth and gave her a kiss. He did remember Sarah, and at the thought, she melted. So they brought him home and released him into the paddock to get adjusted. The next day when she walked up to the gate to check on him, he looked up from the very back and ran to the gate. She laughed and talked with him a bit while giving him some scratches in his favorite spots, and he put his head over her shoulder and used his head to pull her in close for a hug and held her tight while he nuzzled her back with his lips. No words were needed at that point. She could feel him, and he could feel her. The bond she felt with him and the love and understanding they shared never went away.

When the soul cries, the universe listens.

Polly Hershey of Flower Mound, Texas, is quite an adept storyteller and will be featured in another story later this book. It is about turtles and tortoises, while this one is about a female mallard duck. One might think Polly was born under a water sign.

Reunited

SOME YEARS AGO, POLLY WORKED in an office located on a golf course, which sounds like a place where I would enjoy spending my working hours. Their parking garage was carved out of a hillside and was slightly underground with easy access to the outside.

One bright, sunshiny day when Polly arrived a little late for work, she heard a loud commotion coming from the front entry doors she had to go through. The noise was being made by a male mallard duck. Polly said, "He seemed to be trying to get some help but didn't know how to ask, or maybe nobody cared. I looked around the parked cars and found his mate. Her foot was injured, and she couldn't walk very well. I went upstairs and heard he had been there for the entire time people were entering the building." Polly told her boss she had to go home and get a cat carrier, so she could help the duck.

Polly retrieved her cat carrier and headed back to work. When she arrived, a fella who had grown up on a farm offered to help her capture the injured duck. Even though her foot was badly injured, she still managed to evade capture for quite a while. It is amazing what fear can help you do sometimes. Eventually, her coworker managed to round up the duck and Polly loaded her into her car and drove to a wildlife rehabilitation veterinary hospital that she had frequented in the past. Through the veterinarian, she learned part of the duck's foot had been bitten completely off, probably by a snapping turtle. When you read her other story, you will see this is a bit of a plot twist.

The veterinarian had to amputate one of her toes and trim some webbing. He kept her for ten days in order to give her a run of antibiotics and then removed the stitches. During the time she was at the vet, her mate stayed at the parking garage, close to the front door. He quacked imploringly at anyone who walked by. He wanted to know where his mate was and when she would be back. After six days of never leaving the front door where he had last seen her, hunger and thirst drove him back to the pond. But it did not quiet the sad honking sounds he was making. His heart was breaking, and he didn't care who knew it.

Four days after the male had retreated back to the pond, Polly got a call from the vet saying the female duck was ready to go home. Polly and a friend headed out to get her after stopping at the feed store for duck food first.

Polly said the following after arriving back at the parking garage: "Back at the building, we walked her in the carrier to the lawn where the pond was. We opened the carrier, and she stepped out and let out one loud *quack*! We immediately heard her mate calling back to her. He came out from under the bushes from our left and quacked while *running*, flapping his wings, and catching air! And she did the exact same thing, running and flapping and catching air and quacking the whole way. It looked just like an ending to a romantic movie."

They had a few yards to cover in order to reach each other, but they sure did it quickly. The male immediately led her to the water, and in they went. Polly and her friend threw duck food to the other ducks and to the two reunited love birds, and everyone ate happily.

One of the most amazing things was this: The female couldn't swim in a straight line. Losing part of her foot and her rudder on one side meant she would be listing to starboard until she could relearn how to swim. It would come in time, but until it did, the male duck swam right beside her and kept her in a straight line. If that isn't love, what is?

Polly left a bag of food in the guard shack so they could feed the ducks on weekends, while she and others fed them on weekdays. After about a week, the two ducks simply disappeared. A conversation with the vet cleared up the mystery. He said the male duck probably moved her to a less populated pond on the golf course.

Polly would eventually learn that it seemed like every time she is delayed while traveling to or from work, she discovers an animal in distress. I personally think she is in tune with the universe, and when the universe needs something done, it delays Polly, knowing she will be looking for something to help. Thanks, Polly, for your willingness to help those without voice.

Becky Hall of Etna, Maine, can tell you a little about horses remembering things from their past and showing emotion about them. Being witness to this happening with her horses Maverick and Emmy made her a firm believer.

Maverick and Emmy

THE STORY BEGINS WITH EMMY. Becky met Emmy the summer between sixth and seventh grade. Emmy was a camp horse at Oceanwood in Ocean Park, Maine. Becky describes Emmy as "a delicate little bay, with a perfect little star and left hind sock; she was mostly Arabian with maybe a little something else thrown in. I leased her from the end of August until the end of May for three years. As soon as summer was over, we'd move her close to us for the fall, winter, and spring, and then she'd head back to camp once school was out. I lost my privileges to get her back after I made some extremely poor choices my freshman year of high school. We took her back to Oceanwood in May 1996, and I remember how solemn and heartbroken I was saying goodbye to her."

Becky saw Emmy several times over the next few years and would visit her every time she got the chance. The camp had sold her when they closed down. She was in her early twenties when Becky saw her for what she thought might be the last time.

Around ten years later, in January 2017, Becky saw a rehoming ad on Facebook with a picture of a little bay mare. She said the picture looked like Emmy, and when she read the description (a deep voice and petite body), there was no room left for doubt. It was Emmy! She couldn't believe Emmy was still alive. Emmy had to be around twenty-nine years old and had experienced a rough life. Becky went on to say,

"I called the number in the ad and spoke with the woman who owned her. She'd rescued her a few years before and had nursed her back to health. She and her husband were moving to Florida but had agreed they wouldn't go until they found the perfect home for Emmy or until she died, whichever came first. Fast-forward a month, and I brought Emmy home to live out her golden years with me and my very special Morgan gelding, Maverick."

The trip home was not as uneventful as Becky or Emmy would have liked. During the drive home with Emmy, Becky encountered a freak snowstorm that caused a little loss of control of truck and trailer. After regaining control, she pulled off the road to check on her charge, only to find out she had fallen in the back of the trailer and was down. Becky said, "After several failed attempts to stand back up on the slippery, wet rubber floor, Emmy made it clear she was done trying to stand, and we were going to have to figure it out without any help from her. Luckily, she was only about 13.2 with a petite frame, and with four people, we were able to drag/push her out of the trailer and into the parking lot. Once she was on solid ground that had some grip, she looked around, stood up, and walked back on the trailer! At that point, I knew she was definitely meant to be home with me and my other horse, Maverick."

Once home, Maverick went off the charts with establishing his dominance and was completely nasty to Emmy. He spent their early days together pushing her all over the place, especially away from feed and hay, and was "just an overall dingus to her." Emmy gracefully and calmly embraced her role as Maverick's whipping post. He would run and buck and rear and squeal at her. She would look at him, turn the other direction, and slowly saunter off, as if to say, "Whatever, Buddy." After a few months, the harassment slowed down, and they began to coexist fairly peacefully. When Becky would shut Emmy into the barn at night so she could slurp down her old horse hay pellet slop, Maverick would park himself in front of the door, and they would often groom each other over the door. The political pecking order had been established, and now a friendship could build.

After almost a year of making wonderful memories, finding peace in the company of others, and having the best life possible, things took a severe downturn. A week before Christmas 2017, Emmy colicked. It wasn't a bad case, and after Becky successfully pulled her through, she really thought that she would be able to enjoy her company for at least one more winter. Then she colicked again a few days later, and Becky knew she would be lucky to get her through the holidays.

Becky said, "On Christmas morning, in a blizzard, I went out to feed, and found Emmy down in the barn, clearly in pain. She told me it was time, and with shaking hands, I called the vet. She was reluctant to come out in a blizzard on Christmas morning, but I assured her it was absolutely necessary."

Maverick milled around the whole time, and had full access to the barn. When the vet came, it took 150 cc of phenobarbital and more than twenty minutes for Emmy to die. Becky had never witnessed a euthanasia like this one, and it was awful. Even the vet was surprised. I have witnessed just such events with horses when being euthanized, and there never seems to be a reason, but I agree it is hard to watch.

Becky said, "Once she was gone and I'd spent some time with her, we covered her with a blanket and headed inside the house. It was -10°F, and we knew she'd be okay in the barn. There was no way we would find someone to come move her and dig a hole on Christmas Day and in sub-zero temps." As it turned out, it took her nearly four days to find someone who would come at *all*. Emmy remained in the barn during this time. Maverick would wander in and sniff at her, occasionally gently pawing at her blanket. Becky prayed that this extra time with

Emmy would help him to understand she was gone and allow him to grieve a little less once they buried her.

When they were finally able to get her out of the barn, Becky put Maverick into a different pasture, so they could freely work and open gates to get Emmy out. With a few hours of hard, cold work, they nestled Emmy into the ground behind the barn. When all was finished, she opened the gates for Maverick to come back to the barn. With anxiety and trepidation, she watched as he wandered into the barn looking for Emmy. He walked out, looked around, checked the barn again, and with a sudden realization that she was gone, he exploded from the barn with screaming whinnies and galloped the perimeter of the property.

He galloped and screamed, galloped and screamed. Every few minutes he would stop and listen, on full alert, choking on air, with nostrils flared wide, eyes even wider. After a few seconds of trying to hear her, he would be off again, screaming and running, running, running. It was still -10°, and Becky choked on her own sobs as she was filled with terror that he would hurt himself or get sick, and she'd lose him too. These episodes would happen for a few hours; he would rest for a bit, and then the whole scene would begin again. For the first week after Emmy was in the ground, Maverick continued this heartbreaking scenario. Becky would awake in the night to hear the ground thundering under his frantic hooves and his desperate screams, begging for his herd to come back to him. When he wasn't running and screaming, he would post himself at the corner of the pasture that looks down the driveway toward the road. Head up, ears alert, nostrils and eyes wide, he would wait, hoping Emmy would come up the drive. Becky spent as much time with him as she could. She tried to calm him, to help him grieve, to do *anything* that would help him move forward, short of bringing another horse to him, which just wasn't an option at that time. Her heart and soul were completely smashed with grief for her boy.

Over the next few months, Maverick's frantic behavior slowed down. His screaming gallops became fewer and further between and eventually stopped altogether. What *didn't* stop was his post in the corner of the pasture. Humans became his herd, and every time a car came up the driveway, he would whinny loudly and wait at the fence for whomever was visiting him next. Becky felt his grief lift slowly, although she knew he was lonely.

He remained by himself until May 2017, when a friend brought her mare to live with him. They assumed their positions, figured out who was boss, and are together to this day.

Becky was blessed to witness and understand what many others have seen and misinterpreted. Maverick missed his friend. Horses and other animals remember; they feel sadness, love, contentment, peace, and other sensations we humans are capable of feeling. Maybe even more deeply. I know what I believe.

The greatest gift you can give
is what you leave behind when you go.

How long does it take to establish a connection between like species? Can the connection exist unseen or unnoticed by others? I will attempt to answer those questions in this story about Chex and Friend, two horses that live with my friend Kim Thomas at her horse rescue in Texas.

Chex and Friend

KIM HAD RECEIVED WORD a local veterinarian was trying to help one of his clients find a perfect home for her eleven-year-old paint gelding. Lauren, a friend of Kim's, went to see the horse as a possible choice for her mother. Lauren said that Chex made quite an impression on her. He had a sweet personality, rode well, and was a looker. He was also a tall horse, standing at sixteen hands. His height was the deciding factor for Lauren, as he was a bit too tall for her mom to manage.

Hearing the story, Kim and her son Andrew went to meet Chex. Kim said, "We listened to his story as he nuzzled us. His eyes were bright and expressive. We could feel his amazing kindness but also sensed a bit of fear, apprehension, and sadness." In Chex's previous life, he was owned by an elderly woman in Oklahoma who rode him on trails and even along busy roads. His current owner had purchased him nine months earlier to be a trail horse. Time and circumstance have a way of making us change plans. Due to circumstances beyond her control, the owner was not going to be able to keep him because of residential rules about the number of horses a person could have on site. She made the decision to sell him but planned on being very selective about who and where he went.

As a twist of fate or the universe would have it, another horse named Friend became available at the same time. Friend is a twenty-one-year-old gray paint gelding. He had a bit of a rare color referred to as a ghost paint. He looks solid white in the winter, but when he sheds his winter coat, you can see his paint markings. Kim found Friend to be "a sweetheart! He would give kisses and shake each front leg on command for a treat." Lauren decided to take Friend home as a possibility for her mother.

Both horses loaded easily into the trailer even though it had been many years since Friend had left the ranch he was on. Kim and Lauren had asked if the two horses were buddies that should be kept together, and they were told no. They left and dropped Friend at Lauren's and took Chex to Kim's ranch at Pilot Point, Texas. The report on Chex was that he generally stayed at the bottom of the pecking order as far as herd dynamics went, so he was put in a paddock by himself. He would be able to nose over the fences and see other horses but not interact yet. Chex would become very anxious every time the herd horses moved away from the fence to graze. He wanted to be part of something other than himself. Horses are consummate herd animal and need the presence of other horses close by.

Friend turned out to be a good jumper, and standard fences could not keep him in. If he wanted to find you, he would start jumping fences until he could get an eye on you. He really seemed to need human contact, as well as contact with the herd. Some horses are like that. A decision was made to relocate Friend to Kim's ranch and see how he would be with Chex.

When Lauren arrived with Friend, what happened was nothing short of amazing. At Kim's ranch, there is a main gate that stays closed unless a vehicle is coming through. Shortly after Lauren's truck entered through the gate, the talking started between Chex and Friend. By some sense that horses possess, whether it be a feeling of the heart or the ability to distinguish others by individual smells, both horses began calling to each other as soon as the truck and trailer crossed the gate path. Kim said, "Friend joined Chex in the paddock. The horses began rubbing and grooming each other. They ran around the paddock together. When they stopped, they made sure they were touching each other. They ate hay together, shared grain from the same bowl, and slept nose to tail touching at all times. They were so happy."

The more everyone watched these two interact, the more they realized they were a bonded pair, and the information they received earlier had not been correct. Kim said had they known the two were bonded, they never would have split them up. Friend became Chex's protector as they were moved into a herd setting. The alpha of the existing herd, Romeo, started out chasing Chex, but Friend put a quick halt to that action by coming to the rescue. After being corrected a few times, Romeo gave up, and the horses started getting along as a new herd. Kim said, "Every time a horse comes or leaves, the herd dynamics change. We let the horses tell us what they want. We would never have separated Chex and Friend if we'd known they were a bonded pair. It makes our hearts happy to see our horses happy."

To this day, the herd is still intact. Chex, Friend, Romeo, Oscar, Luke, and Generator live a life of peace—a life where none of the horses have to worry about where they are going to live or how they are going to be treated. They don't have to get concerned about the horse slaughter market or the abuse, neglect, or abandonment that their brethren have to endure daily. The Kims of this world are doing their part.

You can't put a value on the
peace that is felt in the presence
of an ageless friendship.
Old souls just know each other.

The Art of Communication

NYTIME YOU TRY TO CONVINCE people animals are more evolved
than we have been led to believe, you must at some point convince
them animals have a way to communicate with species other than
themselves. It is obvious to anyone who observes animals that they
communicate with each other, but what about other species? The first
time I witnessed the phenomenon, I ended up writing "And They All
Said Goodbye" in the book *Unspoken Messages.* It is still to this day
one of the most spiritual experiences I have ever had. I get goosebumps
simply by thinking about what happened that day. After the book
was published, I made contact with others around the world who had
mirrorlike experiences themselves, and the good news is they are willing
to share their experiences. Maybe, between us, we can convince others
of the depth of soul possessed by animals. We know they surpass us
in the senses. They can see better, smell better, and sense danger with
more aplomb than humans have mastered or recognized. I do think we
possess the same abilities but have left the abilities hidden far back in
our psyche, unrecognized and unused.

To be brief, and for those who have not read *Unspoken Messages,* I
will provide a short synopsis of the incident. An extremely well-bred,
smart, and kind horse named Buffy had to be put down. She had a
six-week-old foal at her side. I witnessed the communication between
her and her foal just before the shots were administered. With the
first shot, nineteen other horses that could not possibly see what was
going on started a tremendous din of whinnying, running, snorting,

and rearing. The noise continued until Buffy took her last breath and then stopped as if a switch had been thrown to off. Were I the only one to witness the magic take place, I would have been concerned about my sanity, but there were five other people present who witnessed the same thing. It was absolutely mind-boggling. I was there and confident enough in what I witnessed that I didn't need validation but received it nonetheless.

You do not have to be in the presence of an animal for it to communicate with you, as Jody Rentner Doty of Gig Harbor, Washington, learned. It was an early fall / late summer day in September when tragedy struck in a way you would never expect but which, in reality, happens far too often. The following is her story about the loss of her golden retriever, Kelly. It is a tragic story with an upbeat finish.

Communications from Kelly

JODY SAID, "MONDAY MORNING WAS like so many—hurry up, get ready for work, pack lunches, get the kids up and dressed and into the car. That's when I heard it—the unidentifiable noise that brought me to my lowest point. I had backed the car into Kelly, my fifteen-year-old golden retriever. I didn't see her, and with her aging hips, she just couldn't move quickly. The rest is a blur—a vague recollection of two construction workers hearing me scream and gently lifting my injured dog into the car and then the words from the vet: 'I'm sorry, ma'am, but with her age and condition, she's just too old and broken to fix. It happens more than you know.'"

Jody referred to Kelly as her unconditional love. She was always there for Jody; she was also a nana dog to the kids and a friend to each member of the family. Even their new kitten was adopted by Kelly, who let her nurse on her elbow. Kelly was much more than a dog to Jody and the whole family; she was pure love.

Jody took her kids to a friend's house, came home, and collapsed on the couch. Uncontrollable tears streamed down her face. She cried for hours until she felt something wonderful that changed the focus of her day. She saw Kelly's beautiful face appear before her and, even better, felt her energy. Kelly told her it was her time and not to be sad. Jody asked her, "Yes, but did I have to be the vehicle of your demise … literally?"

Her question was answered with the most indescribable feeling she had ever experienced. She likened it to being held in the palm of God's hand. A warm wave of love filled her body, washed over her face, and instantly dried her tears. Jody beautifully said, "It was peacefully calm, unconditionally forgiving, a love so powerful it transcended all human emotion. I smiled. I couldn't help it. I suddenly felt joy on this, the worst day of my life."

Jody reported that even now, after all these years, she feels Kelly watching over her. Her spirit is a beacon of light that reminds her daily of the power of love and the gift of forgiveness.

What a beautiful story of love, forgiveness, and peace. After talking to Jody about Kelly, I discovered this was not the first time Kelly had shown the ability to communicate over distance. Jody told me of one other instance of Kelly's seemingly telepathic abilities.

Jody said, "I had an experience at work where I had an excruciating headache. It lasted for hours. I took Tylenol, used a cold cloth, but nothing worked. Finally, I took a break from my legal assistant job and sat outside on a bench. It was quiet, and being an empath, I asked God, 'Is the headache really mine?' Immediately, I saw my dog Kelly's face. I thought, *Poor Kelly. She has this headache.* Then, just as it had suddenly appeared, my headache disappeared."

When Jody got home from work, Kelly trotted up to the car. She almost didn't recognize her. Her head was swollen to three times its normal size. Jody said, "Drop it," thinking maybe she had something in her mouth since Kelly was prone to bringing her gifts of socks or toys. She gave Jody a puzzled look as if to say, "This *is* my face, Mom." It turned out she had gotten into a bee's nest. Bless her heart. She had reached out to Jody with her message. Sometimes our pets' psychic messages take time and interpretation to get through to us.

Seems to me Kelly was quite adept at sending messages. Gratefully, Jody was open and on the right wave length to receive messages from her. All of us could learn from this experience. If you sincerely believe in possibilities and are open to things being different than what you were taught, you too will be in line to receive eye opening messages from the universe.

Intuition is not merely a feeling
you experience, but a
message being sent.

Since I started my journey with cancer, I have been blessed to meet many other souls who share my view of the magical universe in which we reside. Lisa Prosen is one of those inspirational people who are open to seeing what most people miss. We discovered a commonality early on. She had experienced cancer and was the caregiver for her father who was suffering with the dreaded disease Alzheimer's. My wife and I were experiencing the same with her father, who passed in August 2018 after two extremely difficult years. Lisa was going through a rough patch one day when she had an encounter with some otters that brought her back to a place of peace.

A Message from the Otters

LISA SAID, "I HAVE LIVED in Palm Beach County, Florida, for almost thirty years now. I have seen the landscape here change drastically. What was once mostly a rural area with abundant farmland is now home to an ever-increasing number of strip malls and *big* luxury malls. I currently live beside one of the busier hospitals in the western part of the county, which is directly across the street from the newest luxury mall, in an apartment for the first time in many years. I lost my home. The reason I no longer have it isn't relative, except to say if I chose to, I could feel very sorry for myself."

To the average American, her situation was rather good, but there was a time in the recent past when she owned land of her own. There was a spot on Earth that was hers alone. She shared it with her family, of course, but they had a place they could always call home. Now, she is a renter.

Lisa shares her apartment with her son, Alec, and two dogs, an aging Maltese named Cosmo that is her most longtime loyal friend and Puzzle who is a black and white cockapoo that is well known in town for his enthusiastic personality. They are, without any doubt, her best companions day in and day out. On the morning this story began, Puzzle gave Lisa the poopy face that is her signal to take him outside or else. It was a beautiful morning, and Lisa gladly got up and said the magic words: "Wanna go outside?!" She was met with great joy by Puzzy, and Cosmo got up and stretched his achy old bones, deciding he was going to join them. On that day, they chose to travel along the canal that is not really part of the community but so close that it is very convenient and a path they often walked on together.

Lisa regularly saw blue heron, various storks, and egrets. Turtles, some extremely large, would occasionally be sunning themselves on the banks and she would catch glimpses of them before they nervously jumped back into the water. They would spot fish, frogs, and many different species of ducks and lizards all around them as the dogs would sniff and pee on every other bush or blade of grass. Every day they enjoyed a different view. Some days were unforgettable, though, and they would see something magnificent and rare. This was one of those days. The otters were back.

A few months previously, her friend Pete was sitting outside on their small balcony taking in the warmth of a Florida winter. Excitedly, he called out for Lisa to come outside. He pointed across the canal at two wild baby otters. Lisa didn't realize otters were wild there in Florida, so to see them in their element was very interesting. It was after a long rain, and they were rolling on the sandy bank of the canal. She had seen them on occasion since then, but they were always elusive, swimming ahead of them as they walked and frequently popping up for air and a quick look back to see if we were still there ... annoying them.

Lisa backtracked a moment and said she had experienced a particularly emotional week. She'd had extreme highs and lows all week, and it was wearing on her. She was dealing with the illness of a close family member, and her career had offered her an opportunity that would possibly change her life for the better. The week was a study in contrasts. Now it was Lisa's favorite day of the week, Sunday, and she found herself especially introspective.

She liked to talk with God on her walks. Her mind would whirl, noticing and reflecting on the week ahead and where she has been the past week. Like all of us, Lisa wondered, *How can I attract more of this or less of that?* Was she content and satisfied, or restless and irritable? She wondered if the goodness she was experiencing would continue and if she were being useful. So when she saw the otters, she was immediately filled with this "*overwhelming* feeling of *well-being.*" As they walked that day, the young otters swam beside them. They looked up and spoke their little otter language to her. She was overcome with the peace of a loving God and knew all was well. The message was they were there to calm her busy mind and bring peace to her day. After all, if you are watching otters play and communicate, your mind has little time to think of other things. It was as if her mind focused on the now instead of being caught up in the past and future.

They had walked much farther than they usually do, so she decided to head home, but first she had to prepare herself to walk away from the otters, feeling grateful for what those little furry creatures had already given to her. She motioned for the boys to turn around, and to her surprise, the otters started swimming with them again. Maybe they were giving her a double dose of peace of mind.

Lisa said, "The smaller one that was leading the way found a fish and jumped quickly from the water with his prize in hand … err … mouth. I was stunned as he scurried and disappeared into the brush that borders this yet undeveloped field. I sensed a powerful feeling of wealth and prosperity coming from the otter. The fish was *big*, and he was feeling very fortunate in that moment. Then, I wondered what the other otter would do in his absence."

As they continued toward their little haven in the middle of town, the dogs were tired of the walk and were obviously excited to go back inside and drink fresh water. They were perfectly okay with all that had happened. They never seemed alarmed by the otters' presence. Lisa watched the remaining otter as it continued to swim in circles beside them. It was as if he was communicating that the amazing sense of well-being she felt was not going to leave her. The season of giving would continue, and she could relax and enjoy what was so graciously being offered to her. The shame and guilt that once plagued her days had lifted, and she was free to enjoy forgiveness and joy. In the midst of what resembled an urban nightmare, nature found a way to communicate, and Lisa found a way to listen. Gratitude doesn't quite cover all she felt. She will always remember the experience as the day the otters walked her home. The next day Lisa found the baby otters sitting outside her apartment door even though she had left them at the canal. It was decided they had been abandoned or lost by their mother, but the story ends happily with them being fostered by a wildlife sanctuary.

I am grateful every single day for the transformation I went through after being diagnosed with cancer. My eyes were opened to unending possibilities and power without limits. I was able to see what most pass on by because of their busy lives. Lisa's encounter happened because she was open to seeing it. I am also grateful for all the friends who share these amazing stories with me. May you become one who sees without being challenged by health issues or tested by the challenges of a loved one. Who knows … Maybe the universe will send you a couple of otters with messages to relay to you alone. I know I am filled with gratitude for the otters being messengers of peace and calmness on a day Lisa needed both.

I am not what I was when this journey began.
I am what I became after life's
lessons were learned.

I have known Lisa Broughton of Gainesville, Texas, for several years, and she is a charter member of my Texas Connection Tribe. When I first met her, I had no idea what she did. I just enjoyed the company of a deeply spiritual person and the in-depth conversations we had. It wasn't until much later that I discovered she was an intuitive and an animal communicator.

She told me this story, and I just knew it would be a good fit for this book. If you have ever watched John Edward or Theresa Caputo on television, this is the same kind of story but with animals as the subject instead of people. And yes, validation is possible as you will soon see.

Meet DeMar

DeMar was a thirty-year-old gelding who was blind and not doing well at all. He had arrived at Shadow Creek Retirement Ranch located in Sanger, Texas, and was under the care of Dr. Deanna Chamberlain. Dr. Chamberlain was the one who contacted Lisa to help with the case. Relaying only the basic information behind the reason for the request, she asked for help. Lisa never wants to know anything else about the animal's background—just the basics. Lisa's role is not to interfere or diagnose disease but to feel what is going on and convey that information to the owner.

By the time Lisa arrived at the ranch, DeMar was pacing his stall, walking the four corners in a constant circle. He said he felt beside himself and terribly worried. She initially thought it was because of his new home, not knowing where he was or what was going to happen. She felt he needed out of the stall so they could start talking.

Lisa said, "I typically start a session by using angel music, and I do use sage to do smudging and to cleanse the area where the horse is to be evaluated intuitively by me. I like wash stalls because horses are comfortable in the stalls, and it's familiar to them. While I was smudging DeMar, I was talking to him the whole time, telling him who I was and what I was doing. We connected immediately. I started by placing crystals on his crown, and I could feel the white light entering the horse's crown chakra. This is where I could see the pictures in my mind's eye that DeMar was sending to me."

DeMar told her about a mare that was left at the equestrian barn back in Massachusetts. Lisa said she could see this was a bay mare, and she was running down the fence line, chasing the transport bus. DeMar told her this older mare was DeMar's seeing-eye mare and his best friend. He also said he was worried because his friend colicked after he left because she was so upset.

Dr. Chamberlain was writing all this information down as Lisa spoke the words. What they learned would be provided to Crystal, DeMar's owner, who was not at the ranch that day. Crystal is a pharmacist, and they were still very busy with their transition from Massachusetts to Texas.

Next, DeMar preceded to tell Lisa he usually ate a mush every morning—a mush of cooked carrots and raisins in oatmeal to be exact. It sounded very decadent to Lisa, but Dr. Chamberlain dutifully wrote that down too. DeMar went on to tell Lisa his picture used to hang on his stall door in his previous home. It was a picture of him jumping a wooded jump, and it was very important to him. He said it told the other horses he was special; he could do things in life, and he wasn't always blind. He also said when not getting mush, he liked his food watered down because it was easier on him that way. All this was written down for the owner. After their first session, DeMar's breathing was calmer, and he was not as worried. He finally had someone to talk to and make his worries known.

This part needs to come directly from Lisa: "Dr. Chamberlain contacted Crystal to let her know about all the things DeMar told me during our session. Crystal was absolutely blown away; it turns out DeMar indeed received a mash every day, and the old mare did run down a brown wooden fence to chase the transport truck. The old mare did colic, and she did recover. The picture of DeMar on the stall door back in Massachusetts was of Crystal's daughter. DeMar was an Appaloosa jumper in his day and a winner. Crystal dug through her boxes and found the picture of her daughter jumping on DeMar, and she hung that picture in the new stall in Texas. It was a sigh of relief for DeMar; he was very happy."

Lisa revisited DeMar a few weeks later because he was still having some problems navigating the stall and was bumping his head on the walls. Dr. Chamberlain installed some pool noodles and bells to help him know where the boundaries were, and that helped.

DeMar became happier, knowing he had someone to communicate with who understood him. He was eventually let out on pasture with the rest of the horses, and he had one horse that was his new seeing-eye horse. DeMar went on to live to be almost thirty-five years old, and his last years were happy ones.

Lisa closed with this: "Horses, just like you and me, love to communicate. They love to feel heard and understood. They also like to make decisions. Each horse has its own personality, and they are willing partners if they are given the chance. There is an energy force for all beings, trees, animals, people, and objects. It is a life force energy, and it can be read from miles away. Horses are sentient beings, and they are intuitive enough to feel for themselves. They can very clearly communicate with you and me. Be open, be of heart, and be kind."

I am so rich to be surrounded by this tribe of people who believe in the magic surrounding us. Learn from the Lisas and DeMars of this world. It is possible to communicate between the species if you know how to go about it.

I have finally and gratefully learned
that I have much yet to learn.

Leslie Jane Peterson and I met in Bangor, Maine, and during our initial conversation, she told me a story about a cardinal and the death of her mother. I am grateful she decided to let me tell her story.

I am from the South, and I grew up listening to the tales of my parents and, through them, my ancestors. I was told cardinals were considered one of the most spiritual of the signs you could receive from the animal kingdom. Visits from a cardinal were akin to visits from a departed loved one. When you spotted one or one made repeated visits, it was a loved one from your past letting you know he or she is still there in a manner of speaking. It should not seem odd then that I hold cardinals in high esteem and see them as messengers from beyond the veil. Cardinals are found in both North and South America. They are also the state bird of seven states in the United States.

Cardinal Visits

LESLIE STARTED THE TALE BY saying, "It had been a week since Mom had passed. The months preceding had been amazingly wonderful and equally devastating. A vibrant, artistic, funny, annoying lady had life ripped away from her. It was time now to return to Maine to start life over without the person who ultimately proved to be the most loving, unconditional supporter ever. Everything was a blur. How do I return to the normal routine of busyness, accomplishment, and daily intentions?" Being one who has experienced the death of loved ones several times, I can feel the loss and pain of longing in Leslie's words.

Leslie told me that the first evening back in Maine, the tapping started, and it has never stopped. She heard a small and light tapping on the window of the double doors that faced the river flowing by. Tap, tap, tap, and then silence. She described it as rhythmic and paced. It was three taps and then silence. In a flash of brilliant red, the cardinal would arrive and tap out its message—three taps, silence, flutter, flit, flutter, flit, again, three taps. In the beginning, the tapping was twice a day, at early dawn and again in the evening, each and every day. On weekends, Leslie found the early tapping to be somewhat annoying, as it arrived when she was wanting to take advantage of not having to arise early for work. She also had been awakened in the dead of night. Her feelings changed from annoyance to wonder. The nighttime visits became thoughts that her mother might be afraid of the darkness and woods. She found it to be the cause of a smile when she heard it arrive, no matter the time of day.

"The sweet pecks continue, in succession, day in, day out. I wonder how my heart is encouraged by the visitor and how I am inspired to look for peace. The predictable, exact, gentle, sweet beats from the beak of a midsized, brilliant red bird. Though hesitant to truly think of such dimensions, I wonder, is this Pop Pop reminding me to be disciplined, save money, and think of slower, easier times in a small Virginia town where cardinals fly the skies? Doubtful. Time has passed for those encouraging tones. It startles, then calms me, the tap, tap, tap continues, always in sequence of three, always interrupted by swooping swirls and twirls."

For two years, the taps were daily and sometimes twice a day. Then their frequency changed, and the visits lessened. Leslie said they "come periodically. I can hear them occurring in the same place, in the same small corner square glass area where the surface has been nicked by the multitude of beak pecks. Sometimes, I whisper, 'Hello, I am doing fine,' as I giggle."

No other bird visited this particular window, just the red cardinal. One thing was constant. The cardinal always visited on the anniversary of her mother's death. The weighted sound of each tap and flutter became recognizable as a visit from her mother.

Her message is interpreted as: "Tap, tap, tap … You are *not* alone. You are strong, day or night. You have parts of me with you, and I created three capable people who will carry on the work that I started. Tap, tap,

tap, swirl, twirl, swoop, tap, tap, tap. The sweet sound resonates, and I am content."

Through Leslie and others, I learned the stories told during the spring of my life were the same stories told to many other people. It became a part of who we are forever. Call it lore, folklore, wisdom of the elders, insight, or intuition. I, for one, think it matters not what you call it as long as you develop a way to actually feel the words deep within your soul and not just hear them with your ears. When the message is felt, it changes you into something more. It brings the power of knowledge and a sureness concerning your future direction. Close your eyes, and see with your mind. The vastness and power of the universe may initially shock your senses, but that shock will change into a peaceful feeling each time synchronicity visits you.

This story about another experience with animals and communication comes from Pamela Cingano of Beaverton, Michigan.

"It was early spring, another of many cold Michigan mornings. However, it held promise of spring ... the promise of better, warmer weather ahead that all Michiganders count on. The evidence of spring could be seen and heard."

Protected by Bud

PAMELA BOUGHT BUDWEISER ON THE same day her younger sister, Andrea (Andy), bought Rags. Bud is a 15.2-hands-high, stocky quarter horse, chestnut in color with a beautiful white blaze that ends in a cross on his muzzle. Rags, a strikingly beautiful Arabian, was 14.2 hands high. He also had a beautiful blaze and sported three white stockings.

Andy had been looking for an endurance horse and found out the farm also had another horse for sale. She called to tell Pamela about Bud, and they went together to see him. She had looked at Rags earlier that day and decided to buy him. When Pamela walked into the barn where the owners had Bud saddled and ready to ride, she fell immediately in love. He was nothing like her vision of the horse she thought she wanted. Pamela had not owned a horse for nearly twenty years, but when Bud looked at her as she walked up to him, he put his head down to smell her hair, and she could hear him breathing in her ear. The deal was sealed; Bud was hers. Eventually, Rags would live with her too. But that's another story.

On the morning of the story, it was five thirty, and the boys had finished their grain. It was time to lead them out to the pasture, which was a short walk of about fifty yards and across a driveway from their barn. Pamela led Bud out of his stall, across the yard, and through the

73

gate. The pasture is about twelve acres of pure mid-Michigan beauty. There is a big old red barn and silo playing sentinel to beautiful old maple and pine trees. A creek runs through the pasture, and on the other side of the creek the woods are heavy and deep. The creek empties into the beautiful Middle Branch River.

Bud was usually as sweet and unflappable, or as bomb-proof as they come—except on that day. He was fine until he walked through the gate and she took the lead rope off him. He walked over to his hay pile, took a bite, and lifted his head very quickly, nervously looking around the area. He started to walk farther into the pasture toward a wooded area, spun around, and dashed back to Pamela and stood there. She thought at the time he must have been spooked by the deer who travel through the pasture and take refuge there in bad weather. She talked to him while petting him, assuring him everything was okay. Just to be sure Bud didn't leave the pasture, she fastened the gate; normally she wouldn't have done that, as he loved his food and would never leave a hay pile.

She put her curiosity aside and walked back to the barn to get Rags. She put the rope around Rags's neck to lead him to the pasture to be with his partner. Bud was high-prancing around the area where the hay piles were, and he was visibly nervous. He was stomping his front feet, snorting, and acting in a way Pamela had never witnessed before.

She unlatched the gate and led Rags through. Bud rushed over to them and stood there, stomping, snorting, and throwing his head around. He would prance away, and if Rags and she moved any farther into the pasture, he would come right back and stop them. He was clearly keeping them contained. This continued for five to eight minutes. Rags and Pamela were just spectators at this point, watching Bud's odd behavior.

Bud finally settled down, and she let Rags go; he immediately headed for the hay pile. Bud went to his hay pile and would take a couple of bites, lift his head, look around, then stare at the wooded area. At the time, she dismissed it as Bud being a big baby about some deer spooking him. However, she also remembered thinking he had never reacted to deer that way before.

Pamela later shared her experience with her sisters and coworkers and heard their theories about what might have triggered Bud's unusual behavior. It wasn't until she had a conversation with her nephew, who was a woodsman in every sense of the word, that an aha moment hit her. They were talking about the dead ash trees he had been cutting down on neighboring property. When she told him her story, he smiled and said, "Aunt Pam, I have seen several tracks where a bear has been crossing the river."

Pamela said, "I will never forget the scene that played out that morning. Bud was protecting us. My horse either saw, smelled, or just sensed danger and he was protecting us—his two best friends."

Like me, Pamela feels a deep sadness when she hears someone say they're just dumb animals when referring to any animal. Bud protected Rags and her that morning. Who was smarter that day? Pamela could never have smelled a bear, seen a bear in the dark, or sensed that kind of danger. She said, "Left to my own cleverness, I could be dead now, which, honestly, is a fear of mine in early spring when bears wake up and are hungry. Instead, thanks to Bud, I'm alive to tell this story."

They lost their sweet Rags the following winter to colic. For a week afterward, Bud would walk over to the grave, smell the ground, lift his head, and look around. Three years later, every once in a while, he will still go visit his friend's grave. They sometimes go together, and Pamela speaks Rags's name so Bud knows that she hasn't forgotten him either.

I appreciate Pamela agreeing to be interviewed and her willingness to share her deeply held feelings and beliefs. I know I believe, just as she does; her horse was protecting her that day.

> It has long been my contention that horses are old souls
> with much magic about them. They have the ability to
> teach and touch those who are open to the gray that lives
> between the black and white lives we sometime lead.
>
> — R. D. Rowland, *Unspoken Messages*

Another person I talked to is Trish C. Giffen. Trish owns an equine rescue and told me about a horse she rescued who initially had a handful of phobias but in time became her most trusted partner.

Trish told me she had recently been asked, "Why did you decide to start a rescue?" The question made her think, and she decided to share her answer with me for this book.

Beautiful Beauty

"BEAUTY. SHE IS THE REASON I started this rescue," Trish said. She dedicates what she does to her. Beauty is her thirty-year-old mare. She got Beauty twenty-six and a half years ago. When Trish brought her home, she was the most untrusting horse she had ever met. She was terrible to work with; the first time she tried to ride her, she was tied to a hitching post, and when Trish came out of the tack room with her saddle, she startled Beauty so bad that she sat like a donkey and then pulled the hitching post out of the ground and was running with it. Once Trish stopped her, it took almost two hours to saddle and bridle her. (Now she knew why Beauty was all tacked up and in a stall waiting when she went to look at her.) Trish was so upset she started making calls, first to the lady she got her from and then the previous owner. This man didn't know she had bought her already. He warned her not to buy her, saying she was crazy. Then he openly admitted to tying her to a tree with a long chain and beating her because "she had an attitude." When he finished telling his story, she got the name and number of the person he bought Beauty from, told him off, and left in a hurry.

Trish's journey of discovery continued until she located the original breeder and owner. Trish said, "Through many contacts and phone calls, I finally located the original owner. She owned both Beauty's sire and her dam. I went to her house, and she was the opposite of those who shared Beauty's life journey in the in-between. She was a very kind person. I met the sire, but the dam had passed away the year before. Her sire was a beautiful gray Arab, and her dam a palomino Morgan."

After talking to the breeder and gaining knowledge of Beauty's life up to that point, she realized it was going to be a long road to gain her trust, and they had many things to work through. But Trish wasn't going to give up on this mare. The first time she clipped her bridle path was quite a treat. Beauty broke cross ties, halters, and lead ropes. Trish remembered thinking she was not only very strong but also very stubborn. So, to show her ingenuity and to show Beauty she couldn't win and she could do the job without hurting her, she went and bought cordless clippers, saddled her up, hopped on with the clippers, and away they went.

Trish felt like she had to show Beauty she couldn't escape and she wasn't a quitter. Two hours and several laps around the pasture later, she was clipped and was no longer afraid of the clippers. It was well into three years of having her when she felt Beauty finally and truly trusted her. They bonded and now have a relationship that is unbreakable. Beauty taught her so much about horses, and Trish showed her that "all humans are not evil." Trish feels like Beauty has protected her and would never leave her if she were hurt. She also helped her train dozens of horses over the years.

Trish told me, "I can talk to her; she listens, and she doesn't judge. More than that, she understands me. If I am having problems with a horse, I say, 'Beauty, talk to this horse and tell him/her to behave.' And she does it. That's right, and many people have witnessed it over the years."

Beauty has had nine foals and has shown Trish the love a mother has for her young. She has proven to her (and her vet who never thought this was possible) that a horse can have maternal instincts. She has raised eight orphans and came into milk for each one. She will let any baby nurse, including even a goat and a dog. Trish feels there is no end to the love showered on others by Beauty.

Trish believes there are too many horses out there with an untold story like Beauty's. You might be left wondering why your horse behaves the way it does. The lesson here is you shouldn't just assume a horse is bad because it is behaving badly. It could have had a past that was traumatizing, and you just don't know. How do you figure it out? Ask … That's right. Ask your horse! Listen to what they are telling you. Watch their body language and how they look at you, how they respond to certain things. This is how they talk to you.

For example, Trish might ask Beauty about the behavior of a rescue. Why is he scared, or why does he buck and rear? She gets her answers too. That's right. Beauty talks to her. It sounds crazy, but it is true. She has been told some pretty sad stories about the horses she gets, but answers come through their eyes and Beauty's. Trish said, "This is why I do what I do. This is why I opened my heart and my home to these beautiful animals and started my rescue."

This is Trish's story. She wanted to add this mare has been her inspiration and has made her who she is today. Beauty has shown her a strength she never thought she had. She showed Trish she can do all the things she sets her mind to and how to look fear in the face with no regrets. Trish went on to say, "I believe anyone who suffers from PTSD, anxiety, or social anxiety should be partnered with a horse; this is truly the best therapy in the world."

Trish has learned many lessons from her roll of the dice several years ago. Horses have a past before arriving in your life. Learn their past, and you learn that horse. Communicating with them is not only possible but, more than likely, probable. The starting point is to know what and where they come from. Once they see you are open to communication, the flow of information begins in earnest.

As a rather sad addendum to this story, Beauty passed away only twenty-one days after her thirty-third birthday. But she did experience a grand birthday celebration, complete with carrot cake and a party hat.

Death is an illusion created by man out of
a fear of the unknown. Freedom is knowing life
is but steps in the constant cyclic
transition of energy from physical to spirit.

Hank Wiley grew up around horses, thanks to his father, Bob, and grandfather, Jake. Both of them had also been longtime horse people. Hank's story follows the adage that if you listen to a horse, there is no end to what they will tell you. It is always best to listen when they communicate, and you need to listen seeking the answer, not by having the answer in your head before the question is asked.

Saving Stormy

HANK TOLD ME, "WE HAD a colt named Stormy. He was born in the middle of the night in a horrible thunderstorm. After some time, he had health issues and needed to be stalled for a few days. Dad gave him thick, plush bedding and lots of hay. The next day he became very ill, and the vet was called. I do not remember the diagnosis, as I was very young, but Stormy was given an antibiotic, and Dad gave him more hay and more comfy bedding."

Apparently, it wasn't quite enough. Stormy got worse. The vet was called again, and this time they were informed there was nothing else that could be done. Hank's father could either have him put down or make him as comfortable as possible until the end came. They put more bedding in the stall and returned Stormy to his temporary home. The next day he was worse yet again. Hank's dad decided to take him out to the barn lot to let him enjoy a little warm sun before his eventual passing.

After a few minutes in the barnyard, in his dad's own words, Stormy went apeshit and started running around the feed lot as happy and healthy as a young colt should be. What had happened? Did he have an allergy to the bedding or hay, or was it simply a horsey miracle? Hank was kind of inclined to believe it was the bedding or being stalled hurting his spirit. But Stormy was *never* stalled again and remained happy and healthy. Hank said, "My take from this episode is that often when we think we are helping, we are instead hurting. And to let a horse be a horse, a dog be a dog, or a person be who they are."

I know from my state of mind, I agree with Mr. Wiley.

Up next is a humorous incident Karen went through as a child. Karen's father had her riding a pony when she discovered horses can not only communicate, but they also have a sense of humor.

Pony Humor

KAREN SHARED, "MY DAD MADE me ride a particular horse. It was a Shetland pony as I recall, but to me, at about four or five years old, it was tall and imposing! It was a grumpy, stubborn animal in general, and I got the feeling it wasn't in the mood for riders, but my dad insisted all my sisters and I ride that day. I was the last rider."

The pony broke into a run and stopped short very suddenly, throwing Karen right over its head. She remembered being shocked. It hurt, and it knocked the air out of her. She was just lying there right in front of the horse, wondering what happened and trying to catch her breath.

The pony was just standing there looking at her ... It could have easily run over her or stomped her, but it didn't. Karen said, "It looked down at me on the ground, and it grinned real big, and I could swear it was laughing. Like, of course, not a human laugh, but a horse laugh. That pony was laughing at me—I knew it. It thought what it did, stopping short and throwing me over its head, was very, very funny. It was grinning and laughing at me, feeling very proud of itself for pulling off this slick trick. I knew it."

Karen told her dad the horse was laughing ... Of course, he told her it was silly and impossible because horses don't laugh. Even at her young age, she somehow knew differently. That horse was definitely amused and laughing at her as she was lying on the ground. Her dad forced her to get back on the pony, old-school and farm-raised as he was. She did not want to. She was petrified and ticked off at the pony, but her father insisted, and you know what they say about fathers and daughters. She got back on and took a spin around the grounds until her dad let her finish.

Karen said, "I got off, walked away, and never got back on. Every time I saw that pony in the future, it side-eyed me, and I side-eyed it back. That horse and I had a *moment*. It remembered. So did I."

I know from my past experience with the animal world that animals do indeed have a sense of humor and quite an understanding of our emotions. I would have loved to have met this character.

Let your smile be the light to show others the way.

Laureen Rideout from Maine is one of my Facebook friends. When she found out I was writing another book about animals, she contacted me to share something she witnessed with one of her dogs and her son Trevor when he was about two years old and had just started walking. Read on about the steps animals will take to keep their charges safe.

Protecting Trevor

LAUREEN STARTED OUT TELLING ME about the day. She said, "It was a warm and sunny morning in Maine in 1977. It was just before lunch, and we were all outside in the backyard, my husband, me, and our two sons. Our two dogs were also with us. They were an older border collie named Bonnie and our year-old Saint Bernard called Ginger. My husband was working on a vehicle he was painting a mural on, and I was working in my garden."

Her youngest son, Trevor, was just starting to walk and was toddling around with the dogs. Her collie Bonnie was always watching the kids, and Ginger was learning from her to be a good guardian. They had purchased Ginger the previous year, a few months after their son was born. They were the same age and growing up together. As she was working in her garden, she occasionally looked up to check on the kids. Her oldest, Jason, was playing with his cars, and Trevor was with the dogs, heading for the garage. He still was not very steady on his feet since he hadn't been walking that long. He would walk a few steps and then fall on his butt.

About five minutes later, she noticed Trevor was crying, so she stopped what she was doing to check on him. He seemed okay, but she decided she might want to keep a closer watch on him. As she watched, he got back up and headed for the garage once again. He walked about ten feet, and Ginger got up and stood in front of him. She is a large dog and was standing in his way, completely blocking him from going into the garage. Trevor attempted to walk around her, but she wouldn't allow it. He tried again but fell down. This kept on for a while until he got so upset he started to cry again.

Ginger just stayed by his side and tried to comfort him by licking him. Laureen decided Trevor must be tired and hungry, so she took the kids inside to feed them. While eating lunch, she discussed Ginger's actions with her husband, but they couldn't figure out what she had been doing.

After the kids finished their lunch, she put them down for their nap and went back outside, still bothered by what happened. She continued to think about the incident, trying to figure out Ginger's actions. Admittedly, they were strange, and Ginger had never done anything like that before.

Later that afternoon, Laureen's husband, who had completed his work on the truck, called to her from inside the garage and asked her if she would mind getting him the broom and dustpan. She asked him why, and he said he forgot to clean up the broken glass off the floor from the day before. He had broken the windshield of the car he was working on, and the garage floor was covered with small pieces of safety glass.

That was when she remembered what had occurred earlier that day, including one thing that had previously escaped her memory. She remembered earlier that morning, Ginger had gone into the garage and cut her paw on the same glass debris. Her husband and she agreed they had solved the mystery of what Ginger was doing; she was protecting Trevor from cutting his feet too. Laureen said, "I've never seen a dog so young be such a good babysitter."

I believe people should embrace their truth and reality, but I sometimes think they miss the magic of existence by limiting their reach to facts and not feelings. I do know what I believe; I believe without a doubt Ginger was keeping Trevor from cutting his feet like she had done earlier. Honestly, I believe I enjoy my reality's explanation a lot better than the other possibilities, but then again, I love magic.

Sometimes, belief is all we need.

This next story is about an amazing experience Jodie Swain of Wilbraham, Massachusetts, had in 2001. Jodie owned an American saddlebred mare named Valley that she bought when the mare was five years old.

Valley of Death

JODIE SHARED: "I'D OWNED VALLEY for just over a year when tragedy struck my family. I received the call no one ever wants; my oldest sister was found passed away in her house. I don't know how to describe the emotional devastation that call caused. My older sister had called me that awful Friday, and she was gathering my parents and asking me to come to her house."

The next few days were a blur for this close family. On Wednesday, after the burial services had been completed, Jodie found time to get to the barn, also known as her peaceful place. She called ahead and asked if she could visit, knowing it was past normal hours. She really needed some peace and to smell the magical scents of the barn horse lovers know so well. The owners knew the reason without asking and told her to come on over and stay as long as she would like.

Jodie walked into the barn and down to the end of the aisle—a walk repeated by habit like she always did. Like animals, humans are creatures of habit. Valley was facing the back corner eating hay as Jodie opened her stall door. Normally, she would have tossed her a glance of acknowledgement and then turned back to her hay. But this day, as Jodie opened the door, she turned to look, and just as she was about to turn back, her face changed completely. Her eyebrows went straight up in a combination of confusion and, more markedly, worry. Jodie felt as if Valley was asking her in a very panicky way, "What happened?"

Valley, who was reportedly as aloof as a cat, turned around, walked up, wrapped her head and neck around Jodie's shoulder, and forcefully pulled her body into her chest and held her there. Jodie said, "That single act of kindness, worry, and empathy opened the flood gates for what turned out to be an epic, cleansing, sobbing weep."

Valley stood there ignoring her dinner, holding Jodie, pressing her into her chest while she wept a soul-washing shower of tears. Jodie covered Valley's neck in tears and snot and cried the big, sobbing tears of someone who is completely broken. She never let go until Jodie had no more tears. When she left the stall, Valley stood right at the door with that worried face while she closed it and then watched her walk completely out of the barn before she went back to her dinner.

Jodie said, "That was the night she truly became my best friend. My best friend is twenty-four years old now. We have had many experiences over the years, but this one charted the course for the rest."

There are many studies that report on the ability of animals across all species to feel what you are feeling. If you are sad, angry, frustrated, fearful, or anything else for that matter, they feel it too. Even better, they react to your feelings with empathy. Horses in particular are being used with boundless success in helping veterans who are diagnosed with post-traumatic stress disorder (PTSD). If you are in need of kindness, understanding, and compassion, visit your animal friends and soak up the peace.

Some of the best conversations I've ever had
were with my horse.

Communication between species seems to be a pretty common experience with us humans. This story is a bit different but relates to communication nonetheless.

Lost in the Forest

LET ME ASK YOU A question. Have you ever been lost? I mean hopelessly lost and frightened straight to the edge of panic? I have been, and I hope to never experience it again.

I was almost twenty-two years old when I returned from Vietnam. I had grown up in a family where we hunted and fished and used everything we harvested. It was a way of life and one I embraced totally. Something happened to me, and the end result was I lost all desire to hunt or kill. I hold no animosity toward those who hunt; it was my personal decision to stop.

Stopping hunting did not change my love for the woods and nature. I admit it took me a while to feel comfortable in the forest again, but I finally did. I would join my friends, people I grew up with, for weekend hunts. I would don my hunting clothes, take a loaded gun, and join them for a day of hunting. I never told them I had no intention of killing anything, and they would hear me shoot occasionally. I always missed because I would shoot five or six feet behind the squirrel so I never hit one that way; I just scared them. On this particular day, we were squirrel hunting in some woods I believed I was very familiar with. We split up and went our separate ways.

I got seriously caught up in watching two squirrels play a game that appeared to be tag. They would rapidly chase one another through the treetops. Eventually, one would catch the other, and there would be some contact. Then they were off to the races once again.

Well, I followed them relentlessly, alternating between watching where my feet were going and then looking back up to the treetops, laughing under my breath the whole time. Their antics were hilarious. This went on for about an hour before I somewhat tired of watching and decided to give them their peace as a way of thanking them for the show.

I sat down for a minute to soak in nature's energy and see what else might interest me. It was then I discovered nothing looked familiar at all. I had never seen this portion of the woods before. Panic considered sneaking in, but I brushed it off and started backtracking in the direction I thought I had come from. About thirty minutes later, I discovered I was back where I had started, having completed a perfect circle of travel even though I thought I had walked a straight line. Panic edged closer as I repeated the process with the same results. I had no idea where I was and no idea how to get back. After the second trip, panic finally set in, and the fear was real. My breathing became rapid, my heart pounded, and my thoughts sped by too quickly to gather them in. I remembered the last time I felt panic, and my mind raced even more. I ended up back in time in a terrifying place.

While hunting, the sign for a hunter in distress is three rounds fired in rapid succession. Those I was hunting with heard the shots I fired, and one returned the message the same way. I was able to get a direction setting from the noise and eventually made my way back to him, relieved when I reached a point where things were once again familiar.

Upon making contact with my fellow hunter, he asked if I had been lost. I replied, "Nope, I was shooting at two squirrels and missed them both." Yep, to save face, I lied. Hope he doesn't read this book.

Now keep in mind I was in my early twenties. How would I have reacted if I were eleven years old? How about nine years old? Well, this is what happened to Linda and Patrick McNulty, siblings from the piney woods of Camden, Arkansas, who were those ages respectively when they had their experience with being lost.

They were part of a large family consisting of the mother, father, two sets of twins, Patrick, and Tiger, the star of this story. The day Tiger became a member of the family was described as the happiest day of their lives by young Linda. Tiger was a mix of collie and who knows what. He had long hair and a collie-like appearance but with shorter legs, a blunted nose, and a bit of a spaniel appearance added to the mix. He was initially named Sandy because of his coat, but their father said he looked like a tiger, and the name stuck.

Tiger never received any formal training; he was simply a member of the family. He had a way of seeming busy when nothing was going on. If the family returned after any length of time, he would chase off some imaginary trespasser with his hackles raised and a ferocious bark. He would then return expecting praise for taking care of the place, and he generally received it.

The family home sat on federal forestry property in the middle of thick woods and hidden from prying neighbor eyes. It was in these woods that Linda, Patrick, and Tiger decided to embark on a hike one beautiful day. They walked through familiar areas and crossed familiar fences without a care in the world.

Then they heard a noise they had never heard before. Off to their right was a huge forest of pine trees. It was windy that day, and they had never heard the whispering of the pines before, so they quickly became entranced with the sound. The ground below the pines was covered with pine needle sheds. Otherwise, the ground was clear and the walking easy.

As they walked, they stared up at the crowns of the pine trees, watching the movement of the treetops and listening to the whispering wind. They sometimes turned in circles and sometimes walked straight.

They turned left, and they turned right. The crowns appeared much like one of those childhood kaleidoscopes that most of us have received at one time or another. It was completely mesmerizing, and they lost any sense of direction they may have at one time had.

When I was lost in the woods, I was in my twenties. I know what true panic feels like. Panic and I have had an intimate relationship ever since Vietnam. I know! What I cannot imagine is being eleven and nine years old and having that same sense of hopelessness.

Linda and Patrick had no idea where they were or which way led home. There was no path to follow, and they left no signs in the carpet of pine needles to lead them back out. Linda admitted to both of them being terrified, but they managed to remain calm.

Anxious to find a way out of the woods, they looked at Tiger, and their racing minds came up with a plan. They both decided to see if Tiger could get them out of their predicament. It seemed the only way out was through Tiger, so with hopes he understood, Linda simply said, "Tiger, let's go home." She said he gave her such a funny look, right in the eye, and just that quickly, he turned and started walking. He looked back once to see if they were following.

Both Linda and Patrick never doubted Tiger would lead them back home, and I believe a lack of doubt ensured home was exactly where they would end up. The universe is like that. After thirty minutes of walking through unfamiliar territory, they gratefully arrived at a barbed wire fence known to both of them. There, just beyond the fence, was the path to home. Panic was erased as if it were never there. Success just has a way of negating panic.

Needlessly to say, Tiger got a bunch of loving that afternoon, and he ate it up. He was loved in the beginning, middle, and end of his life. It is heartbreaking animals live such short lives, isn't it? Tiger lived to be nine years old. Linda was a sophomore in college at Southern Arkansas

University when she developed the flu and had her mother come to take her home to heal. When her mother picked her up, she delivered the news of Tiger's passing. She told her he was perfectly healthy one day, sick the next, and gone the day after. His passing was peaceful.

Tiger was buried in the woods he loved so much. They were his playground and now his resting place—a place of peace in the magical world of nature. He left a trail of broken hearts and a river of tears in his wake, but he also left smiles, laughter, and memories of life's youth. All these many years later, his memory is as alive as it was that day in the piney woods of Arkansas. Good dog, Tiger. Good dog.

It is by being lost that we become found.
Lost is a period of discovery, both inside and out.

I wrote earlier in this book about Jennifer and me moving to Maine to care for her elderly parents, but prior to this, our summers were a mix of time in Kentucky and time in Maine. Jennifer would spend most of each summer at her parents' house. I would usually head up in late June or early July and stay a month.

It was during one of these periods of separation when a mallard duck we named Scooter came into our lives. At the time she was a small, hatchling-sized powder puff, and she was totally lost.

Scooter and Jennifer

D URING OUR SUMMERS IN MAINE, Jennifer and I would take advantage of downtime by visiting some of the many lakes in the area, either for swimming or kayaking. On this particular day, I was still in Kentucky, and Jennifer was in Maine. She had decided to escape the heat and go swimming at Tunk Pond. It was here she first spied the little puff of down that would later become known as Scooter.

Scooter was all alone swimming in the pond and quacking repeatedly, loudly, and without letup. It was obvious the hatchling was in a panic. There were other people at the pond, and Jennifer asked them about the duck. She was told that it had been there quite a while by itself, calling out continuously. Jennifer possesses a heart full of love for animals of all species, so her attention became focused on the small, panicking bird.

One of the funny things about this story was Jennifer's attire. Of course, she had on a swimsuit, but over it she was wearing a T-shirt from the American Society for the Prevention of Cruelty of Animals (ASPCA) with a cartoon caricature of a dog and a cat. Jennifer talked to everyone there about the possible location of the duck's family, but no one had seen them. One kayaker returning from the pond said he saw some ducks around the point swimming away. He went back in an attempt to herd them back to the beach area without success.

After an hour or so of watching, worrying, and investigating, Jennifer sat back and continued to keep an eye on Scooter. Well, either feeling the vibes or seeing the T-shirt, the little duck came out of the water, waddled up toward her, and crawled under her bent legs. Scooter then proceeded to lie down in their shade and fall fast asleep. Jennifer waited another hour while the duck slept, hoping beyond hope for the return of the family, but that never happened.

We are taught to leave baby animals alone with the hope the mother will return, but in almost three hours, no other ducks were seen. It appeared that if she got up and walked away, it would be a death sentence for Scooter. Jennifer did what any big-hearted animal lover would do, and she cradled the new addition to the family in her T-shirt and left for home. It was time to research raising ducklings.

Little did Jennifer know she had just become the adopted mother of this duckling. It was a role she not only relished but also excelled at. Scooter followed her simply everywhere she went. She had an aquarium to sleep in with a light bulb for warmth and plenty of bedding. She also had a couple of swimming pools so she could swim several times a day. Scooter had plenty of food, both cornmeal and meal worms, that she loved to dive after. Her favorite time of day was early evening because she would get on Jennifer's shoulder, burrow under her hair, and go to sleep while enjoying the comforting warmth of another being.

Scooter loved to hunt slugs in the yard. While she was hunting, Jennifer would go about her yard work and inevitably get out of Scooter's sight. When Scooter would notice, she would panic and start quacking loudly and running around wildly trying to find the only mother she knew. Once Jennifer was located, she would settle (after a few choice words about being left alone) and begin hunting slugs again.

Scooter spent the entire summer with us and was well on her way to becoming an adult duck. What we were feeding her must have been working. We had plenty of advice on how to care for her. Jennifer had also checked with a local duck rescue initially to see if they could raise her, but they were full, and it would be quite a while before they could take on another project.

As the summer was winding down and a return to Kentucky was being planned, we knew we had to make a decision about Scooter's future. We were not set up on our farm to have a single duck. She wouldn't have lasted very long. Jennifer has a friend with a son who raised ducks for a hobby. They knew about Scooter and offered to provide her with a forever home at their place.

The week before leaving, Scooter was taken to Ellsworth and delivered to Merrill and her son. I'd be lying if I said there were no tears at the handoff because there were ... several. But knowing she would be better off in the company of other ducks, geese, and chickens eased our minds and made the transition simpler. I played only a small part in saving this little creature. Most of the work was on Jennifer, and it was harder on her to let go, but she handed her over, and we closed the book on this story. We received updates and pictures for a while, but life always has other things to occupy our time and minds.

Coincidence does not exist in my world. Everything has a time and a plan, and there is a reason for the little oddities that happen in life. This story was no exception. Look at the facts. A recent hatchling was separated from its family. The little one was in a true panic and had no idea what to do. Remember, it was a wild animal, not a hand-raised member of a family flock. Out of all the people on the beach that day, Scooter picked the one wearing the ASPCA T-shirt and recognized the vibration of a helpful and loving person. She parked under her legs, and that turned out to be a perfect place to ensure her future safety. Everyone is entitled to their opinions and beliefs. I know where I stand.

At day's end, when the dust has settled,
you'll realize true rewards are born
from calmness and compassion.

Kimberly Kearney lives in Mount Washington, Kentucky. She made a connection with a dog who completely changed her life. Because of that connection, the lives of many other dogs were also improved.

Boozer's Story

IN JUNE 2002, KIM WAS privy to a conversation taking place at her veterinarian's office between the vet and his nurse about a dog that had been left tied to a tree on the side of the road in Tennessee. The dog was starved and sick. Intrigued and saddened, she listened to the whole story. The dog, who would later be known as Boozer, was taken in by a shelter, and they had reached out to Denise King of the Louisville Weimaraner Rescue for help. She, in turn, had contacted Dr. Selby, who was the contract vet for the rescue. Kimberly had a long client relationship with Dr. Selby at the South End Veterinary Clinic and had recently lost her first Weimaraner named Duke.

As Kimberly listened, Dr. Selby and Teresa told the sad tale of the abandoned dog. The dog was heartworm positive, but the shelter in Tennessee did not have the funds to treat him, and no one had stepped up to foster him. Adding to these challenges, the dog was so weak and sick, it was highly doubtful he would survive the treatment. Without needed treatment, the dog would surely die slowly. Kimberly heard Dr. Selby say he could do the treatment at no cost if the rescue had someone who could foster him during treatments. After hearing Teresa say that she would work on finding someone to take care of him, Kimberly spoke out and said she would go to Tennessee and get him.

Do you readers see the synchronicities involved in making this a successful rescue? There were so many things that had to be timed perfectly in order to put this cast of kindhearted people in the same place at the same time, and help this animal that was unable to speak for himself. They stepped up and became his voice.

This part of the story needs to come directly from Kimberly's heart:

> Plans were made, and I and my son, who was eleven at the time, left early Saturday morning and drove halfway to Bowling Green, Kentucky, to meet a kind person on that end who had offered to drive and meet us. When I got there and saw the dog, I immediately started crying. This boy was a full-grown male Weimaraner (his normal weight should have been seventy to seventy-five pounds) that weighed thirty-five pounds and was nothing but skin and bones. Yellow-green snot was coming from his nose, and he was so weak he could barely stand. I wasn't prepared for that. We laid him on a soft blanket in the back of my SUV. On the way home he scooted up as far as he could and laid his head between the seats on my arm.

> We got him home, and I fed and cared for him until Monday. Monday I was to take him to the vet's office, and they would start treatment, and he would go into foster care. The president of the rescue called me and said they didn't have a foster home for him, so during treatment he would have to go into boarding. I said I could foster him and take him back and forth to treatment; after all, he had never left my side all weekend. He would hobble to wherever I was in the house and just watch me and lay close to me.

This is the point where I am reminded animals collectively ask for nothing but your company. It is my fervent belief that every animal domesticated by humans deserves to be provided with care and treated with compassion. Kimberly stepped in and did both extremely well. These are the hearts I love and respect.

I have to tell a little aside about the name Boozer. Boozer's name when he came was Gus, and Kimberly found it to be a sad name. Her son was a basketball fan and, in particular, was a fan of Carlos Boozer of Duke University because of his strength as a player. So, Boozer he became. After many months of treatments, Boozer got stronger and gained weight. He became the beautiful dog Kimberly saw inside the emaciated and abused boy she picked up that day.

The decision to adopt Boozer as a member of her family was an easy one for Kimberly. He stayed by her side, protected her and her three sons, got her through a divorce, and not once ever needed a leash, even during a trip to Fort Sill, Oklahoma, for her son's graduation from US Army boot camp. She said it always seemed like he knew exactly what she was saying and minded perfectly. They were so connected that her sons told her Boozer knew when she was turning onto the road home because he would start whining two to three minutes before she got there.

Sometimes six years seems a lifetime and other times a blink of the eye. In December 2008, Boozer became sick and wouldn't eat. A mass was discovered in his stomach, and surgery was scheduled. Dr. Selby called later that afternoon and told Kimberly poor Boozer "was eaten up with cancer," and it was too involved to do anything about it. He was still on the operating table, and his recommendation was to let him go instead of awakening him. It was a very hard decision to make, as I know personally, but Kimberly made the right decision to let him cross over instead of living with the pain he had been experiencing. Kimberly said, "I knew I did the right thing, and that morning when I left him for surgery, I had kissed him and hugged him. He knew he was loved, and I knew he loved me."

Boozer wasn't just a rescue. He was a valued and loved member of the family. In his short six years with them, he taught more than he was taught. It never seemed as if he needed teaching but, instead, instinctively knew what was being said to him. And he paid back love for love for all that had been done for him. Even more importantly, he planted a seed of thought in Kimberly shortly after his arrival. That seed grew into a dream of helping other animals in need of love and comfort. His seeds have grown and will continue to thrive for time eternal, feeding the souls of all animals his family contacts.

From Boozer's presence in her life, Kimberly came to the realization she wanted to do even more to help those without a voice. So, more she did. Thanks to the seeds planted by contact with Boozer, Kimberly has rescued over forty dogs, a few cats, and one pig that had been liberated from a dog fighting ring in Nelson County, Kentucky. That pig came home with her in the trunk of her car on a Super Bowl Sunday. Her name is now Rapunzel, and she is living her life out on a farm in Shelbyville. All these lives were saved thanks to Boozer and the heart possessed by Kimberly—a heart that has her doing what others will not do. And Boozer's energy is felt as if he still sits by her side, where he was always the most comfortable. And he is not just there in spirit, but his cremated remains sit in a place of honor in Kimberly's home.

Words and deeds served from a kind and
compassionate heart, feed the hungry soul.

When writing on the subject of animal communication possibilities, you will never convince Penny Fullerton of Glen Dale, West Virginia, that animals cannot communicate in understandable ways. It was mid-June one year when she had an experience with her guineas she will never forget.

Penny and the Guineas

PENNY SAID, "SOMETIMES WE HAVE to leave the farm and stay all night in town. Before we leave, we always make sure all the animals are fed and the chickens and ducks are put in their house, safe from any coyotes or foxes that might harm them. The llamas and the goats have their own safe place to stay. Our two cats, Red and Fat Cat, usually sleep on the porch of the farmhouse or roam around at night catching mice, and in the winter, they stay in the garage. As is the case with most cats, they do an excellent job of taking care of themselves."

Penny also had three guineas, and they were the watchdogs of the barn yard. Penny told me that from the very beginning, they stayed to themselves. When they learned to fly, they roosted on the roof of the chicken coop.

Nearby the coop was a maple tree they sometimes liked to roost in as well. They would navigate to the roof of the coop and then on to the maple tree where they would spend the night. She never could get them to go in the chicken house with the rest of their feathered friends. They seemed to like keeping an eye on things from the vantage point high in the tree.

Guineas are known for alerting the other animals to any noises or strangers coming their way. So, Penny always felt the guineas were safe at night on the roof or in the tree because they actually were the ones who alerted the other animals of any danger. Beside the coop, they had placed a child's wading pool for the young ducks to swim in. They had a pond but didn't want the young ducks crossing the fields to get to it.

When the Fullerton family had to go to their home in town, they always made sure they came back early the next day to let the chickens out and feed everyone else. It was on one of those clear-blue-sky days when they came home, and Penny could hear the guineas' screeching sounds before she could see them. She said that this time seemed quite different, as the sounds were loud, frantic, and totally out of character. She knew by the way they were acting there was something very wrong.

Penny said, "They were much noisier than they ever were before, and it was then I realized there were only two guineas. As I got out of the car, they frantically ran circles around me, making screeching noises and trying to get me to go up the path where the chicken house was located."

Penny followed their lead toward the chicken coop, and she immediately saw the third guinea lying in the baby pool they had put out for the ducks to swim in. The guineas ran to the pool and were wildly screeching and hysterically moving around. Penny said, "It was a sad, pitiful sound they made, as if they were crying out for me to help them, letting me know what happened while I was gone. As I reached the small baby pool filled with water, I bent over and picked up the third guinea. He was lifeless and had been there for a good while. I held him and was sad to see what had happened."

Penny started to cry because there was nothing she could do. He was gone. Suddenly, she realized it had gotten very quiet. As she looked down around her, Penny saw the other two guineas just staring at her. It was amazing to her that as soon as she touched their brother guinea, they quieted down. She looked at them and told them she was sorry for what had happened to their brother and she would bury him and always remember him. Animal lovers are like that.

As she walked down the road with him to a place where he would be safe until she could bury him, she remembered that she hadn't let the chickens or the ducks out yet. Any other time, as soon as they heard her coming in the morning, they would have been greeting her with their loud clucking noises, but today it was very still. It was as if the whole farm was experiencing the death, and she intuitively sensed their grieving.

Penny went about her day, letting the chickens and ducks out of their house and feeding them, as well as the llamas, the goats, the cats, and the three dogs that had been in town with her. She felt as if they all knew one of the animals was no longer with them. The two remaining guineas didn't try to eat all the chicken feed like they usually did. It seemed as if the whole farm was grieving for the loss.

"That day the guineas stayed in the high grass by themselves, and when they did show up around 6:00 p.m., they were very quiet as they looked for their supper," Penny said.

Penny later buried the deceased guinea. While digging the hole, she thought about what had happened, feeling that knowing would help make sense of the whole thing. She finally decided the guinea must have been on the chicken coop roof and had somehow walked off the edge, falling into the baby pool. Any number of things could have caused him to fall into the pool, but in the end, she couldn't fix the death any more than she could fix what caused it to happen.

Reflecting back on her arrival that morning, Penny was very surprised at how different the sounds were, and it seemed to her they were waiting for her to get there and help them. They effectively communicated to her something wasn't right. They also quieted and became calmer as she reverently recovered the lifeless guinea from the water. "There was no language barrier between the species that day; we all communicated. That was the day I felt the connection," Penny said.

I believe if you are reading this book, you too may have had experiences like the one Penny and others have had. You might have explained it to yourself as mere coincidence or some sleight of hand by the universe, but of this I am sure: you will come to believe differently as the universe continues to show things to you about the truth of life's experience. The lesson will be repeated until you understand it. Thank you for sharing your experience with us, Penny.

Learning is a gift, even if pain is the teacher.

I hope you believe as I do when I say animals have personalities that mimic those of humans. Sometimes they learn by watching us, and sometimes they learn through repeated action. There are those who believe animal personalities run the complete gamut of possibilities. There are good and bad in all species. I want to tell you about a minimule named Jake. His name was added to as his personality was revealed to his new owner, Laura, the owner of Forever Home Farm Sanctuary in Kentucky. After hearing Laura's story, I became a believer that curmudgeons exist in the equine world because Jake certainly seemed to be one.

A Curmudgeon Named Jake

IN THE FALL OF 2016, Laura was contacted by a man inquiring about the possibility of her taking what he called a donkey. The man's son had traded a pickup truck for the donkey and had since moved out, leaving the donkey behind. Laura went to the man's farm and met Jake. She let the man know that what he had was not a donkey but was actually a minimule. She was impressed by what she saw and agreed to take Jake. She told the man to bring him to her farm when he was ready to part with him.

Jake arrived November 16, 2016. Laura had decided to put him in her front pasture with an older horse named Romeo. She did not want to overwhelm him on his first day by putting him in a herd situation. She did a little research on the name Jake to see if his personality fit his name. Jake is a medieval variant of Jack and also a short form of Jacob. Jake got along fine with Romeo, and after two weeks of letting him nose over the fence and generally acclimate himself to the rest of the horses at the facility, Laura decided to introduce him to the herd and let the horse politics begin in earnest.

The day he was put in the field with the rest of the charges, there was the normal running, bucking, and bickering. Once a perceived dominance was established, they settled down but only for a while. There began a cascade of skirmishes, all instigated by Jake. First, he started paying a lot of attention to the oldest jenny in the herd, Lilly. A large donkey named Bo didn't like the attention one bit so he challenged Jake on the matter. He quickly learned that wasn't a good idea. Jake went all over him, up one side and down the other until Bo retreated in embarrassment.

Jake, not being one to quit and experiencing a blood boil over his fight with Bo, decided to expend some energy going after a minidonkey who happened to be the only one smaller than Jake. Well, that didn't sit well with Little Man, a black-and-white walking-quarter horse mix who was the herd boss. Things didn't bode well for little Jake, and he ended up bowing to the dominance of Little Man, but did so begrudgingly, as any true curmudgeon would do. He earned name number two after this little escapade. Fearless fit perfectly!

Giving in to no one else, other than Little Man, Jake went about his new normal. Being number two wasn't so bad, and he had plenty of others to boss around. And boss he did. If he wanted someone else's hay, he ran them off and took it. None of the other horses wanted to experience Jake's wrath. Laura had to keep an eye on him all the time, so the other horses could get their needed feed.

Laura would stand with a whip in hand on days when she fed the horses, not to hit anyone but to make a whoosh noise by shaking it through the air. I own a whip for the same reason, and like Laura, I have never used it on anything but the air. It was an attention-getter, and usually Jake would back off. Somewhere in his life, he apparently had felt a whip and wanted nothing else to do with it.

One particular day, Jake had been trying mightily to get some feed that Laura wanted to go to two other donkeys. She thought Jake had given up and walked off, so she set the whip aside to attend to another of the many chores that inherently come with owning an equine facility. She heard a ruckus and turned around to see what was going on, and what she saw was gut-busting funny. Jake had retrieved the abandoned whip and had set about chasing the other two donkeys away from their feed. The look on his face was priceless. It was a mixture of hidden humor, the kind where you do not want anyone to know you are having fun, and laser-focused determination to get that feed. The donkeys left their breakfast, but Jake wasn't through using this newfound power. Rather than eat, he looked for another target. He found one. With a new burst of energy, he went after Laura, shaking the whip and trying to herd her, much as a cutting horse will direct the movement of calves. Fun is fun, but eventually, Laura got the whip away from Jake, who from all appearances walked off with a mule smile, his chest out and a high step in his gait.

Laura sometimes feels sorry for Jake because not many of the other horses want to be around him. She has told him in talks that he can't treat others the way he does and expect them to want his company. She explained little-man syndrome to him in a way she hoped he would understand, but his bullying still runs full-time. He does follow the others, sometimes from a distance, just for the comfort of their energy. He also now buddies up with the minidonkey, who more or less tolerates him. And such is the tale of Jake Fearless Jacob Jack, who will no doubt earn many new names as his life continues.

It makes one wonder if Jake exhibited learned behavior by picking the whip up and chasing others with it while making the whooshing sound. Or, quite possibly, Jake is a curmudgeon with a sense of humor. I know which side I lean toward.

When it is all over, you will discover it
was never random, and
coincidence didn't exist.

I have written so far about the ability animals possess to communicate with humans and each other within their species, but let's entertain the possibility that communication across other species also exists. I think once you read about the events Kim Thomas witnessed one day while loading horses that had never been loaded before, you just might be convinced of the possibility.

Kim runs a huge equine rescue in Bartonville and Pilot Point, Texas. This event was without a doubt eye-opening for her and those around her.

A Tiny Bird Shall Lead Them

KIM WAS DRIVING TO THE ranch one morning in June 2017. A strange number came through on her phone. She told me she doesn't usually answer numbers unknown to her because almost all those calls are from salespeople. On this particular hot, sunny morning, she answered. Her daughter-in-law's brother had given a friend her phone number. He was trying to help a woman he met find a home for her paint horse herd. Kim was a bit intrigued, and she called the owner for more details. The horses had all been foaled on the owner's property. The overly wet spring washed out some of the fencing on their land, making it necessary for the herd of eight to be contained in an unshaded paddock. They were selling their property and couldn't keep the horses. She knew what often happens to untrained, unhandled horses, so she was trying to find a safe home for them. She could not stand the thought of her horses being sold for slaughter.

Kim knew she shouldn't even consider the thought of taking in eight more horses, but she offered to drive to the owner's ranch to meet them. When Kim arrived, she was glad to see the horses looked totally healthy, but there wasn't much shade or any shelter for them. The family obviously loved their horses but simply could not provide for them

111

anymore. The herd was friendly and beautiful with clear and curious eyes and slick coats. Kim thought she surely could find good, forever homes for them because they looked so good. After six weeks of trying, she realized that was not going to happen. People want horses they can ride. Most aren't able to train them themselves, and these particular horses were not trained.

The horses were getting more and more sunburned under the hot Texas sun as time continued to tick by, and the discomfort of the horses weighed heavily on Kim. It was time for plan B. She had started calling the horses *the painted horses*, and she began making plans to move the horses they'd already come to love to her ranch. Jasper; Hope; Katie and her colt, Twister; plus Cheyenne and Michaela all loaded without injury or drama. She and her ranch hand transported them on two different days about a week apart.

Shiloh, the herd sire stallion and his Medicine Hat daughter, Willow, were the last two left to move. Attempts to load them on a previous trip had Shiloh blowing through the panels of the chute they had made. Willow attempted to jump the six-foot round pen and was caught up in a fence panel. Both escaped with only a few scratches, but Kim knew they were in for a challenge, and they would need a lot of time and patience, not to mention more human power, to bring these two beauties home.

On a steamy, hot Texas day with humidity so high it showed like sweat on your skin, Kim, her ranch hand, and two friends went to pick up Shiloh and Willow, prepared to take as much time as needed to convince the horses to get on the trailer. They backed into the side of the round pen and made a chute to guide the horses. They had feed, alfalfa, apples, treats, and an abundance of patience. Over a two-hour period, they were able to shrink the confinement area and move the horses closer to the trailer. Gratefully, everyone remained calm.

The horses were starting to examine the trailer. Kim wondered if they were thinking about how their family members disappeared into the same trailer and never returned. Or were they unsure what the big, dark box was? Over the next couple of hours, they moved the panels in closer to the trailer. By this time, the horses' bellies were full of the food they had brought. Kim put alfalfa in the back of the trailer, hoping they would be enticed by it into this strangest of unknown places. Kim thankfully refused to let anyone push the horses or scare them into moving. It had to be their choice to load.

When they reached the point of being completely out of ideas, Kim said she began praying, asking for divine intervention to help them get the horses on the trailer. She soon noticed a tiny bird (a Texas house wren) on the fence beside the trailer. Kim said, "He was chirping up a storm. The horses were munching alfalfa. Tiny Bird continued to chirp. He then flew over and landed on Shiloh. He sat there chirping as Shiloh ate. Tiny Bird then flew over to a nearby tree. He continued to chirp continuously. He flew back to the horses, circled inside the trailer, then landed on Willow. Tiny Bird flew back to the fence and continued chirping."

Then, the most amazing thing happened. Willow lifted her head, and she calmly walked up the ramp and into the trailer. Shiloh calmly followed her. Where did Tiny Bird come from? How did he know they needed help? They closed the doors and drove the horses to the ranch to join their family, where they witnessed a happy herd reunion.

Shiloh and his son, Jasper, were immediately gelded. Twister, who was four months old when he came with them, was gelded the following spring. Katie, the dam of Twister and Michaela, foaled the following May with Oliver, a solid chestnut colt with a star. All nine of the painted ponies reside in beautiful grass-filled green pastures at their ranch in Pilot Point, Texas.

What took place on that day in Texas when it was hot enough to bake cookies in the mailbox? There are those among us who will say it was purely coincidental. And then there are those of us whose faith or belief in prayer or intention is so strong we have no doubt of the power of our thoughts and words. We know that when we put something out, something will come back, and come back it did. I believe the Tiny Bird was a messenger—one who brought a tale of coming peace, of green, grass-filled pastures, of an abundance of needed shade, and, most of all, of a coming reunion with herd mates. All the horses had to do was take a chance at change and get on the trailer. Once the message was received and understood, they loaded, and life for them began anew. That, my friend, is what I believe with all I am. Live long and happy at your new forever home, painted ponies.

> I am awed by the power of nature's
> majesty and her ability
> to silence a noisy mind.

In my journey through this thing called cancer, I have read prolifically to the tune of at least one book a week and sometimes two. I have always felt I was led to read the works of certain authors by some plan of fate. One of those authors who led me out of the pit that cancer drags you into is Eldon Taylor, PhD. Dr. Taylor is a New York Times bestselling author of many books. All of them became a road map for my successful navigation through illness. I ended up communicating with Dr. Taylor, and we have since become fast friends. We shared somewhat like paths through life in that both of us had careers in law enforcement, owned and operated an equine boarding/training/breeding facility, and went on to become authors. We also shared something much deeper—a deeply spiritual experience involving the death of a beloved horse. Eldon has gratefully agreed to share his experience with the readers of this book, and for doing so, I am in his debt once again. The following is a story he shared in his book *Choices and Illusions*.

Horse Telepathy or Spiritual Awareness?

THE STORY AS TOLD BY Eldon:

I used to raise and train horses, and I owned an all-breed stallion station and racing stable. We stood (made available for breeding) a number of stallions, including several of mine. As a result, every year we handled hundreds of mares that belonged to other people. All our breeding was done in hand, which means one person handles the stallion on a lead line, while another one or two hold the mare. Each evening we would tease the mares (test them for readiness to receive the stallion) and breed. Sometimes, depending on the horses, the schedule, and other variables, we bred only after a daily palpation by the veterinarian. The point is that the horses were handled daily and with great care.

One day my foreman came to me about a customer who was delivering his mare for breeding. The horse didn't have the required health papers that I insisted on before animals entered our facility. I went out to meet the customer myself.

I saw the mare standing in front of the barn offices as I approached. She was a beautiful young animal but obviously wormy—bony and with long, coarse hair. A very young filly was suckling her. After exchanging pleasantries, I told the owner that he'd have to come back when the mare hit her thirty-day heat. (He'd brought her in foal heat because the filly was only a few days old.) In the meantime, he should worm the mare, give her inoculations, and get health papers for her.

The owner was quite upset about this inconvenience. He insisted that we should take the mare. I tried to explain to him that she wasn't in the best of health for breeding and that to protect his investment, he should worm her lightly with a paste wormer before tube worming her. Too good a kill of the worms could send an overload of dead parasites down her digestive tract, which is known to cause colic and kill horses.

The owner insisted that he'd made arrangements to bring the mare to us in foal heat and that he'd paid the stallion fee and therefore wanted her bred now. I refused, pointing out that the contract required the mare come to us with current health papers. The owner drove away angry.

He went straight to a vet who gladly tube wormed his horse, gave her shots, and hung health papers on her. This vet and I didn't see eye to eye, so I wasn't surprised to see his name on the documents when the owner returned with the mare and filly. We had no contractual choice at that point but to take the mare and do our best.

Two days later, she was in trouble. I received the phone call at home during dinner. She had colic that was discovered during early evening checks. As you may know, colic is an attack of acute abdominal pain localized in a hollow organ and often caused by spasms, obstruction, or twisting. It's the number-one killer of horses. The intestines become twisted or tied in a knot, and the horse dies of peritonitis.

I instructed that our farm vet be phoned immediately, as well as the mare's owner, and that my employees keep the mare up and walking. I arrived at the ranch to find the vet already there. Soon thereafter, the owner arrived with his entire family, including seven or eight children. The night dragged on as my foreman and I took turns walking the horse. We did everything we could. She was given drugs to relax her and minimize the pain, and we'd oiled her stomach. When the vet left around eleven thirty that night, we knew the odds were against saving her. She'd laid down and refused to get back up. I went to the mare and took her lead line from my foreman. I sat down on the wood shavings that covered the indoor alleyway and arena where she was lying. I lifted her head to clear her eye of the shavings, and after brushing the eyelid and lashes clean, laid her head in my lap. She just looked at me as I gently stroked her head and neck. Her foal was free in the passage not far from us. Some members of the owner's family were around the filly, talking to her and petting her, and the remaining people in the barn were standing near the entrance to our coffee lounge speaking to each other. For a moment, the mare and I were alone, eye to eye, sharing only the helplessness of the moment.

The barn was full of horses. The alleyway separated the stalls on each side of the barn that was 303 feet long and 60 feet wide. The stalls on both sides were twelve feet square, and the horses in the fifty-plus stalls were all turned away from the lights that lit the center of and entrance to the barn. It was midnight and well past their bedtime. I stroked the mare and heard her filly neigh. As I saw her eye roll toward the filly, I thought of how sad she might feel if she were human, and I wondered if she felt that way. I spoke softly to her, reassuring her that I'd see the foal was taken care of. She looked at me, and the breath left her body. Still and dead, her head lay in my lap, and only I knew it, at least as far as the humans present were concerned. For just as her last breath left her, every one of the horses in the barn turned and came forward, leaning their heads over their stall doors into the alleyway. As though on cue, they all began neighing, whinnying, and otherwise setting up a vocal ruckus. Somehow, they knew.

My foreman asked, "What's wrong with the horses?" I told him simply that the mare had passed. I'll never forget that night. How could the horses know this mare died at exactly the moment she passed? She made no sound, and I made no announcement. How did this information reach them? What is there about animals that we don't know? How can we claim so much specialness for humans and know so little about other species? What does that say about being human? I shared this story in my e-newsletter and book, *What Does That Mean?* (a Hay House publication) and discovered that it wasn't one of a kind. Readers shared both their views and some of their stories. Here's just one, as told by Karla:

"Eldon, we had a similar experience a few weeks ago. One of our horses developed a tumor on his head that didn't respond to surgery and treatment. It was encroaching into his mouth and airway, and we could tell he was uncomfortable, so we decided to have him put down. The other horses in another pasture were quiet until I watched our friend take his last sigh. A few seconds later, the other horses started running around, neighing. They seemed to know."

So I am not alone in witnessing this telepathic means of communication that horses use. I hadn't read Dr. Taylor's account prior to writing *Unspoken Messages*. Only afterward did the tribe of others who have witnessed such things come to my attention. I am glad to be in the company of those who have seen and acknowledged the seemingly magical abilities of our equine brothers and sisters. It is real and not a figment of imagination—the true reality of a magical universe where all things are not only possible but probable. A place where things are quite different from the ideals we were spoon-fed since birth. I still think we are born with the knowledge of the power of the universe, but through training, we not only accept the ideologies of others but embrace them as absolute truth. It is only when we become enlightened, either by a life challenge or by something else that deposits us at the bottom of life's barrel, that our eyes become finely tuned to the things which are possible. It is with a sense of regret that I view most who share this world with me, those who fail to see magical possibilities and instead accept science and coincidence as their rulers. Animals defy science and the rules of coincidence if only you will pay them the attention they deserve. Just because they are without voice doesn't mean they are simply dumb animals. Observe without preconceived ideas and ideals and witness the truth.

Originally published in *Choices and Illusions* by Eldon Taylor and reprinted here by permission.

Once a mind opens, it is impossible to close.

Meet Kayla N. Reilly from East Texas. We communicated on social media about her horse, Bob, and I found a quite interesting story to pass onto you.

Bob and Lucy

BOB WAS OFFICIALLY KNOWN AS Mr. Bob Marshall, his registered name through the American Quarter Horse Association. He was a stunning bay gelding that was almost blind. Kayla said, "Bob was my horse. We had a very strong bond, and I had trained him to verbal commands years before. He was always so eager and trusting and would do anything I ever asked of him."

Bob's best friend, protector, and his eyes was Lucy. Lucy was a thirteen-year- old grade mare and the herd alpha at Kayla's farm. Lucy would protect Bob from the aggressive horses in the herd, and she took her job as a seeing-eye horse for Bob very seriously. They were side by side constantly. If you saw Lucy, you saw her shadow, Bob.

In 2013 Lucy had a foal, as did another mare at the farm. Lucy became even more alpha, to the point where she became very aggressive toward other horses but especially toward the other foal. Separation didn't work, as Lucy could get out of any place you put her, and when she did, she headed straight for the other foal. Kayla made the hard decision to sell Lucy because the herd politics just could not be worked out, and the other horses and the foal were in danger of being injured or killed. Lucy left the farm in the late summer, early fall of 2013.

Life for Bob changed dramatically when Lucy left. He lost his guide and protector. His sadness was palpable, and he would stand in a corner, protecting his backside from the others and hanging his head. It did not take long for the other horses to zone in on the mild Bob and make his life miserable. It only added to the depression he was feeling at the loss of his friend Lucy.

Kayla said, "He became a picky eater and lost the spark in his eyes. I watched my once healthy and thriving boy wither away before my eyes. No matter how much feed I poured into him, he continued to lose weight. I took him to the vet numerous times, and he was clinically 'healthy as a horse,' and veterinarians could find nothing wrong with him."

Kayla remembered one day she went out to check on the horses, and Bob was lying on the ground. Her initial though was Bob had passed away, but upon closer examination, she saw Bob was breathing but had no interest in getting up. Even though he knew voice commands, he simply would not respond on this particular day. He lay like that all day long.

Over the next few months, Kayla went through her own set of challenges. She and her husband got a divorce, and he took the mares that had been so cruel to Bob with him. Kayla bought a younger mare who luckily bonded well with Bob, and the light in his eyes came back on. He returned to having a good appetite and ate with gusto. It seemed the new mare knew instinctively Bob was practically blind, and she became Bob's new set of eyes. She was always close by him in case he needed her.

Sadly, a couple of years after finding harmony in his existence, Bob passed away peacefully from a brain tumor. His last years were gratifying for him, and it can be said he crossed over in a much better state of mind and circumstance than he sometimes existed with. I am sure he was appreciative of Kayla for creating a place of harmony for him in his last years. Ride on, Bob, and enjoy not only a return of your sight but also the lush, green pastures of abundance you now live upon. Someday, the others will join you.

Peace is a path you must willingly choose
to travel. It is not one that can be forced upon you
or gifted to you.

Juli Mohan from the Joshua, Texas, area had an experience about horses grieving to share. Juli possesses a large heart when it comes to animals, and she often takes in horses others overlook. Much was the case with the three horses that Juli had when this incident happened.

Sugar Mourns

JULI HAD SUGAR LENA CHEX (Sugar) for eight years before her passing. She took Sugar in because no one else would. After an illustrious career, she was used as a brood mare, and her owners considered her used up. Juli provided a safe harbor for Sugar for the rest of her life.

Also part of the family was Dolly, a big-barreled, impeccably bred sorrel quarter horse Juli had taken over the care of from her mother. Dolly had a grand career on the show circuit. Late in life, she had a bad bout of equine protozoal myeloencephalitis (EPM) that almost killed her and left her severely crippled. EPM is a neurological disease that is spread when horses eat food or forage that is infected with protozoan Sarcocystis neurona.

Rounding out the herd was a third mare named Abby who was in relatively good health.

Sugar was the alpha mare of the herd and kept everyone else in check. Abby was second, and Dolly came in at the bottom of the pecking order. Juli said, "Dolly had the sweetest disposition of any horse I have ever owned and always wanted to please her owners and any of her herd mates. Sugar was very affectionate toward me but bossy to her herd mates, despite her age. She remained the dominate mare until the day she crossed the bridge."

In 2017 Dolly's condition worsened. She was in a lot of pain and discomfort, and the medications that had been working were no longer effective. Without anything new to try, it was decided the kindest thing they could do for her would be to let her go. Dolly was euthanized at home and buried in the back pasture.

Dolly was only eighteen years old when she reached the end of her stay here. Throughout the whole process, Sugar was agitated. Juli had to keep her up and away from what was going on with her friend, and the whole time, Sugar let Juli know she would rather be with her friend instead of being closed up.

The day Dolly was euthanized, Juli had a neighbor bury her in a grave in the back pasture of the ranch. That would be the same grave Sugar stood guard over for more than a week while she mourned the loss of her friend. She would simply and quietly stand with her head hanging low to the ground. Her eyes would be closed for long periods of time and when open would be without focus, just staring off in the distance.

Sadly, last year Sugar, at age thirty-three, joined Dolly once again on the other side of the rainbow bridge after suffering a heat stroke. She is buried beside her friend in the back pasture, but I am sure the two of them had a grand adventure after being reunited by time. I am grateful to Juli for sharing her experience. Think of all we might miss in life if people chose not to see and share the magic.

I hope each of you is able to look back upon your
day and know you made a difference.

Eldon and I are not alone when it comes to having amazing and life-changing experiences with horses at their moments of crossing over. Meet Nicole Pellandini Eubank. Nicole was raised in very small towns in northern California, where she was born into and raised around the horse industry. Her parents owned and operated a horse training and breeding business where they also gave lessons. Although well-traveled, Nicole has never ventured far from her earliest memories of being in a barn among horses. Nicole told me the things she has learned from horses forever changed her life, and those changes started with a once-in-a-lifetime horse. This is his story.

Becoming Pegasus

NICOLE SAID, "AS A VERY young child growing up, I always felt I had a deep-rooted understanding of life, a gift maybe even. I felt things deeply, and I felt the energy of other things around me. This was very confusing for me to feel not only my emotions but also the emotions of other things as well. At such a young age, I lacked the ability to properly communicate it all just yet, but I understood there was an order to things, a proper balance, and that energy was at the core of it all. I understood every single thing was full of energy and that not all energy was good."

Sounds to me like Nicole had a good start on understanding the nature of things at an early age. What a blessing to see and sense beyond the noise that surrounds us daily, especially while in the spring of life. It leaves the rest of life to sharpen those skills.

Nicole found out early that the most beautiful creations in her universe were horses. She remembered spending hours paying homage to the powers that be of hay and grain, imploring them to send her a winged horse to soar around on. Little did she know her wish would someday come as close to happening as reality would allow.

An early event in Nicole's life would plant even more seeds for the future. It was during her third-grade year that her teacher played the movie *The Black Stallion*, and it became her quest to replicate the events of the movie in her life. Yes, she wanted that unruly horse, the one no one but her could ride or touch. Her wishes were about to come true.

At the young age of seven, Nicole decided the adrenaline rush of barrel racing was going to be her focus. She tooled around on her palomino pony, Goldie, and worked her way up to her mother's old western pleasure stud, Sparky. However, her eye never left the prize she wanted. The prize would be her father's solid black cutting horse named Mud Puppy. The problem was no one was allowed to ride Mud Puppy but her father. Would he relent and let his daughter ride him? After all, unknown to him, Nicole's mother would sneak the horse out and ride barrel patterns with him—an experience that still makes Nicole giggle at the memory.

Nicole knew Mud Puppy was her black stallion and her Pegasus, and she had to find a way to convince her father to let her ride him. He always said the horse was way too much for her. Mud Puppy was a reject cutter—a horse too hot-tempered and fired up to calmly walk into an arena without scattering cattle and nipping those who got too close. There was so much energy about him that it was said by other trainers and handlers that he was dangerous and should be handled with caution. Do you think knowing this would stop her wishes and wants? Dreams of the black stallion ruled her thoughts, and she never once relented when it came to wanting to ride Mud Puppy.

In due time, the day to ride came, and here is what Nicole had to say about it: "Finally, I wore my dad down enough, and I guess he figured he had Mud Puppy worn out enough after his workout that day, already unsaddled and walking him around with a halter and lead rope to let him roll in the sand arena, that my dad finally said, 'Okay, Nik Nik.

Here's the deal. If you can lope Mud Puppy around the arena and keep him on the rail bareback with just a halter and lead rope and not fall off, I'll start giving you lessons on him. You have to ride him exactly as I tell you, though. You got it?' I thought if Alec could ride that wild stallion around the beach after a ship wreck in the movie, then this would be a piece of cake!"

Knowing how important this ride would be, Nicole rode him just as her father had directed. True to his word, the lessons began shortly afterward.

Nicole was a good student, and she and Mud Puppy grew into a formidable pair. They started entering and winning barrel racing events everywhere they went. Their winnings were often chronicled in local newspapers. People would comment that Mud Puppy would not let anyone touch him except for Nicole. Together, they broke numerous arena records in barrel racing and pole bending. The future was bright. They didn't even let a broken leg Nicole experienced during her eighth-grade year in school slow them down. Her mom had to put an English stirrup on the left side of the saddle to accommodate the cast. She still has the picture.

Nicole and Mud Puppy qualified for the National Barrel Horse Association finals that would be held in Augusta, Georgia, for the top of 1D in the youth category for California. Sadly, it was a competition they would not go to.

Nicole said, "We were gearing up for the NBHA finals. We were at the peak of our winning and had won so much. While doing our daily workout, Mud Puppy suffered a career-ending shoulder injury. One bad slip on bad dirt left him limping on his front end all the way out of the arena and home. We gave him some pain medication and hydro therapy, but when he was still lame after a week, we hauled him strait to UC Davis. After countless exams, tests, and the seemingly never-ending rehabilitation at home for months on end, we discovered we were fighting a losing battle. Eventually, the injury would be categorized as catastrophic, costing him his life."

To say Nicole was devastated does not quite cover the depth of pain she felt for what was coming and for what had ended. She went on to say, "All my memories, all my achievements that gave me confidence and self-esteem, he was a part of it all. This beautiful horse with so much spirit. He was there when times were good and when times were bad, always listening, always loving me, and always resilient. And now one bad slip in bad dirt, and I had to make the hard decision to say goodbye to my best friend humanely." Her heart was breaking in two.

It was a beautiful midsummer's day—too beautiful for what was about to happen. Mud Puppy was led into the area where the goodbyes would take place, and as he was being led to the head of the rainbow bridge, all the other horses started running and whinnying. The air was electric with an unknown, previously unfelt energy, and all the horses were part of it. Much like the experiences Eldon Taylor and I had respectively, the horses simply knew one of their own was about to leave for other parts and planes. At first, Mud Puppy tried to run with the rest of them, and it was sad to see him try.

Nicole said, "I had to let him go. I had to let my Pegasus return to the sky he came to me from. I had to be there for him. He was not that crazy horse we were told he was. He guarded me with his life every run, every day. His energy and mine were whole together, and I had to say goodbye to the form of his energy I knew and recognized it to be. I know energy cannot be destroyed; it just manifests into something else. I just didn't know what that would be, and I was already missing the form I knew it to be for so many years with him. I found it comforting, understanding his energy would always be here even if I didn't recognize it. He'd always be with me."

Nicole hugged him and said her goodbyes before nodding to the veterinarian. Then, something totally unexpected happened. Nicole felt his soul or energy, if you will, leave his body when he crossed over. She told me, quite eloquently, "I knew without a doubt on that day there is something more than our physical bodies. Possibly the greatest gift I could receive from such a torturous loss is the knowledge that we all go on after this life. When his spirit took its flight from his physical self, I felt it. I do not know where it dispersed to, but I do know his soul left his body. The horses whinnied and continued running crazily in the pastures while the sun was setting. Had it not been such a sad loss, I may have been able to appreciate the beauty of it all the more on that day. I still imagine Mud Puppy's spirit running out of the confines of his failing body, spreading his wings, and joining the horses running in the pasture, and I believe that is why they kept running and playing. He was truly free to be a Pegasus again." A perfect example of the energy of the universe.

Nicole's heart and mind arrived at a point of belief and true faith in what she felt and witnessed. She felt his soul leave. Are you listening? She felt his soul leave. She witnessed the lightness depart his body and leave complete stillness behind. His light left his body but not his place in this universe. All he was is still here to call upon.

The seeds this horse planted inside a young girl grew strong and sure. There was never a doubt where Nicole would end up. She lives in Texas and is a barrel racer, horse trainer, and a breeder of foundation, cow-bred quarter horses and paints. Her husband is Chad Eubank, a recently retired rough stock cowboy who competed in bareback, saddle bronc, and bull riding. He also trains and breaks horses. I guess *break* is not the right word, as what he does is get them to agree on what he wants, all with a light hand and voice. Together, they are quite a successful team.

Much like Eldon and I, Nicole was gifted a glimpse into the enchantment that surrounds us, mostly unseen by all but a chosen few. When I had my experience, it was and still is the most spiritual experience I had ever had. I get goose bumps with the mere thought of what transpired that hot summer day. I am grateful Nicole will have the same powerful memories for the rest of her days. We are proud to be part of the chosen, and we know we carry valuable knowledge with us forever. Just be open to possibilities and question all you have ever known. You might just be surprised when the universe shows you a glimpse behind the veil.

Question everything, but be open
to any truth,
even if it proves you wrong.

Because of what I coexist with, I have spent more than a decade knowing without a speck of doubt that I lead a blessed life. However, I didn't know how blessed until I started the research for this book. I have met so many think-alike people virtually that I am often surprised by the number of tribe members who quietly surround me. For a while, I was hesitant to speak of the things I had witnessed for fear of ridicule and the questioning of my sanity. Now I feel blessed to be able to share so many stories about the amazing world of animals and the magic they bring to our lives while hiding behind the veil separating us.

One category continued to scream for attention and inclusion in the book. This category is split into two subjects: healing and diagnosing illness. Do you believe animals have the ability to sense when something is medically wrong with you? Do you believe they will know before you? Do you believe they will try to find a way to let you know? The people I interviewed are believers.

I met Anne Moran, my friend and cocancer traveler, after *Unspoken Messages* was published. She was dealing with a breast cancer diagnosis, and I was learning to find my way through my diagnosis. Early in our friendship Anne told me how she discovered her cancer had returned, and I knew right away her story needed to be told. She was definitely given a glimpse behind the veil.

The Doctor Is In

ANNE AND I HAD GROWN up in the same community but in different circles. We were acquainted but not yet friends. As I look back after our friendship developed, I wished we hadn't waited so long to become friends. I am forever in debt to Tommy Jenkins for making the introduction.

As it is, she transitioned before me, and there is not a day that goes by that I do not think of her and remember the deep conversations we had about subjects many and varied. I have written before about the love we tribe members feel for each other, and there is none other quite like it. We are collectively understanding and supportive, and we get what others can only wonder about.

Ann was diagnosed with stage two breast cancer in 2009. She went through treatment and thought she was in a lasting remission. Her life was full; she had plenty of energy and was experiencing no pain. Given how good she felt, she went through life accordingly, living every single moment straight out with a beautiful, beaming smile while her infectious laughter trailed behind her.

Anne had a huge heart when it came to animals, and she understood their level of evolvement more than most people. She adopted a neglected Tennessee walker buckskin from a fella who had gotten in over his head and couldn't properly take care of the number of horses he had. Korbel was the buckskin's name, and after she got the pounds back on him, he was a stunner. Anne saw the potential of this spirited but safe horse and knew he was going to be a good addition to her herd. Anne preferred horses with a little spirit and a smart mind, and Korbel did not disappoint her in either category. He rapidly became one of her most trusted mounts. And life, for a time, was perfect.

Unfortunately, life has a tendency to throw you curves when you are expecting fastballs. Sometime in August 2013, on a beautiful late summer day, Anne was in the barn saddling Korbel for a ride when he did something quite out of character for him. He unexpectedly drove his shoulder into Anne, shoving her up against the wall hard and quick. Anne was surprised, and she was also hurting, particularly her hip. She was surprised because in all her time with Korbel, he had never done anything you could even remotely characterize as mean-spirited or dangerous. Before and after that day, he never did anything like it again.

Anne went through the fall months of 2013 in pain and looking for answers. She visited a massage practitioner and a chiropractor but could not find relief for the pain. Worrying and fretting did not enter her mind; seeking answers did. She went to an orthopedic doctor who ordered an MRI of her lower back and hip. The results were not what

Anne or any of her circle wanted. Her cancer had returned and grown into a stage four level. No one, with the exception of those who carry this diagnosis around with them, can know how news like this affects a person. It can feel like being handed a fifty-pound weight and told to tread water … for the rest of your life.

As bad as the news was, there was a glimmer of hope. See, Anne was dealing with a stage four cancer while being asymptomatic. In other words, she had no idea anything was going on prior to being injured because she exhibited no symptoms. The timing of the discovery couldn't have been better given the totality of the circumstances. Had Korbel not bodychecked her into the wall causing a painful injury, she would not have visited a doctor when she did. Because she went to the doctor after being injured, she found out she was eligible for a new clinical trial. Being included in that trial extended her life another two and a half years. Had she not gone to the doctor when she did, the cancer would have continued its march. It would have progressed beyond the point of any successful treatment, and she would not have been eligible for the drug trial.

Can you see the twists and turns the universe takes while we are on this journey? It was a one-time event, and Korbel did his job perfectly. Normally a docile horse with no vices other than a love for life spirit, he became aggressive at the exact moment in time when he could get the results he wanted. He wanted Anne to go see a doctor, and he made it happen.

My friend and sister-in-kind Anne passed away in April 2016. She rode horses right up to the end, and not once did Korbel ever act up again. That job was finished, and his last job with Anne was simply to take care of her until time was up. He knows something the rest of us only wonder about. He knows he will see Anne again, and there is no reason for sadness or longing. Time will see to everything; it always does.

Live an afterlife of magical wonder, Anne. In time I will see your smile and hear your laughter once again, and I will laugh and cry tears of happiness with you.

Sometimes, no matter the handicap,
no matter the challenge, against all
sense of reality, we still embrace hope.

Next up in the category of diagnosing and healing is a friend I have only met on the internet. However, it has turned into one of those friendships where you can be out of touch for months, reconnect, and never miss a beat. Katie Holme and her husband, Ed, own Healing Horses, a nonprofit organization, located between Rock Hill and Lancaster, South Carolina. They are also affiliated with Project HALO. They are dedicated to the rescue, rehabilitation, and offering of sanctuary to area horses that are victims of trauma or abuse.

Kindred Spirits

I F ANYONE WAS FORCED INTO a position of experiencing PTSD, it is Katie. Her suffering continued until she was healed by the heart of a horse named Chief. Meeting Chief and seeing firsthand the magical healing ability of the horse led to the beginning of their nonprofit.

Katie had this to say about her experience: "When horses are focused on their role as healer to broken human spirits, they connect in an unworldly way with warmth, deep understanding, and empathy. Their sole purpose is to bring balance, harmony, and peace to that place in our hearts and souls that is troubled and full of pain. With unconditional love and ancient wisdom, horses save the lives of the most deeply wounded. They are the ultimate healers in this world; this is their unique gift to us."

Katie suffered a trauma many years ago that left her with all the devastating physical, emotional, and spiritually life-changing effects of PTSD. In a desperate effort to recover, she researched and engaged in many traditional and nontraditional treatments. They were all unsuccessful, and her suffering continued for many years. Then Katie experienced an uptick in emotional health when she rescued a horse named Chief. Chief had suffered past abuse and trauma at the hands of cruel human beings, and he exhibited the same fears and symptoms of PTSD that Katie did. He was labeled as dangerous and unmanageable.

Katie said, "We were kindred spirits and had an instant, ancient connection and shared a deep love and understanding of each other. For the first time in many years, I felt a sense of freedom and hope for a brighter future. I began a journey with him to a place of well-being, harmony, and peace. He became my constant riding companion and best friend as both our symptoms of past trauma seem to drift away as we rode for miles together through the woods."

For more than twenty-three years, Katie and Chief went on to rescue and rehabilitate many other equine brothers and sisters. Then Chief and Katie expanded their healing to humans. Together, they established a unique program using rescued and rehabilitated horses as healers and therapists for people who are suffering. Chief healed and changed the lives of many beings. Katie went on to say, "I feel so blessed to have met such a magnificent sentient being. I believe he, like all horses, is one of God's angel messengers on Earth."

Chief went to the rainbow bridge more than two years ago. He is buried at Kate and Ed's Healing Horses sanctuary, and his energy and presence are felt all around them as they continue their mission of healing through horses. Kate wrote a poem for Chief on his passing and has been gracious enough to share those words with us.

To Chief,

You lent me your freedom in place of my fear, and carried me back home to Mother Earth dear.

Where once again I see Rainbows and butterflies bright blue in the light of your truth, I believed in you.

Through your generous spirit you helped me to cope,
replacing the past with the present. Changing fear to
hope.

And now as we heal together with deep love and grace,
our old wounds are healed, gently nursed in this place ...
Thank you my dear friend.
I am eternally grateful to you and will love you forever.
See you at the Rainbow Bridge.

©2017 Katie Holme

Katie and Ed do some amazing work at Healing Horses, and she relayed the following to me about the sanctuary: "Healing is conducted from an equine perspective through a structured program that employs gentle, nontraditional methods. The end result is well-behaved, respectful horses that are confident and at ease. Healing Horses is also committed to helping people overcome adversity of the heart, mind, and spirit by helping them realize their full potential as valuable human beings and showing them a pathway to healing and inner strength through the horse."

The work of Healing Horses is managed and directed by Katie Holme and is made possible solely through the help of close friends, kind volunteers, and the financial support of compassionate and generous individuals.

Meeting people like Katie and Ed Holme validates the journey I am currently traveling. It simply makes the odd and unexplainable very believable. Meeting like-minded people who have witnessed the same type of circumstances I have around animals validates all I have seen and done. It makes me feel a sense of kinship toward all who have seen magic and lived to believe in it.

It is often the quietest person
who hides a thousand feelings
behind the happiest smile.

Cats are also part of the wondrous world of animals and the stories they tell without words. This story comes from a friend in Ellsworth, Maine, named Victoria. She and her uncle witnessed an animal's power to not only recognize health issues in humans but also to do something about it. Babe is the name of Victoria's Uncle Ed's cat. Victoria told me the story might be considered out there by some, but she knows it is what happened on a magical day when she discovered the hidden, fairy-tale world of animals.

Babe's CAT Scans

VICTORIA TOLD ME HER UNCLE rises very early in the morning. Eighty-eight-year-old Ed likes to be at work as the manager of Island Buses by four o'clock in the morning, as he says he gets more done before everyone shows up for work.

On the morning of this story, Ed had risen at his usual time. As was his pattern, he headed to the bathroom to prepare for the day. But this day brought surprises with it. He told Victoria later that when he got up, he felt dreadful and decided to go back to bed for an hour or so and hope for an improvement. He said his stomach didn't feel very well at all.

As he lay down on the bed, Babe started sniffing him. She became very restless and got onto his chest. She started kneading and knitting on his chest and purring very aggressively. Ed told Victoria Babe was actually hurting him. That is not surprising; Babe is a fairly large cat, weighing in at more than fifteen pounds. Ed said she became very aggressive, and she wouldn't stop. For some reason, the message he was getting was she didn't want him to lie down.

When Uncle Ed sat up on the side of the bed to placate Babe, she still wouldn't stop. At this time, Ed suddenly experienced sharp pains radiating down his left arm. He knew then why she was behaving so odd. Ed got himself to the emergency room at a local hospital in Ellsworth and was very quickly transported directly to Bangor, Maine, by ambulance.

Victoria and her mom were right behind the ambulance. By the time they had parked and entered the hospital, Ed had already been taken into surgery. Everyone agrees that had it not been for Babe's insistence, Ed might not have known what was going on and may not have gone to the hospital. Ed remembered his thought at the time was Babe knew something he didn't, and he knew somehow that he had to listen. As things turned out, Ed got there just in time for them to save his life.

"Yes, we all think Babe saved his life," Victoria said. "Uncle is still working, and Babe continues to do regular CAT scans on her daddy. She sleeps beside him every night and watches over him. She is an angel."

Victoria, her mom, and Ed were selected by the universe to receive a peek behind the veil we speak of, and that peek enabled them to see the somewhat hidden yet enchanting world of animals. They witnessed the intuitive side of animals and their ability to diagnosis and, yes, heal. My hope is each of you are able to witness the same world that they did.

There is a magical world of wonder
within each of us just awaiting discovery.

While on the subject of cats and diagnosing, meet Marble, a now-twelve-year-old nursemaid cat from Texas. Marble lives in the barn at the ranch of Jim and Linda Rogers just outside Whitewright, about fifty-five miles northeast of Dallas. The farm is called J-BAR-L Miniatures, and they run a nonprofit called Mini Hooves of Love Miniature Therapy Horses where they take well-trained minis to visit people in need of a pick-me-up. They stay incredibly busy spreading love to those who need hugs, hope, and the smell of horses.

Marble is a cat of questionable heritage who came from a litter of feral cats born in the barn, but there is no question about the size of her heart. They could tell when a mares in foal was getting close to foaling because Marble would take up residence in her stall until the delivery day before giving up her watch to move onto the next mare. As regular as clockwork for about a week to ten days, she would stay in the stall and then exit on the day of delivery. Not as good as having cameras, which Jim and Linda also had, but pretty darn close.

Marble the Foal Whisperer

JUNE 1 DAWNED AS A seasonably hot and dry day in Texas when Jim and Linda noticed Marble had vacated her watch at Carmel's stall, and they knew something was up. Jim discovered that Carmel was in active labor, but something was wrong. The foal was turned wrong and would be a breech birth at best. He knew he needed help and quickly.

The veterinarian was called, but it was going to be at least a forty-five-minute wait. No one had expected a problem delivery, as this was Carmel's fourth foal with no previous problems. Expected or not, Jim had his hands full. He had a lot of help from other breeders who stayed on the phone with him and walked him through the process as best they could.

When you are hip deep in an emergency and find yourself waiting on experienced help, time slows to a crawl. The second hand of the clock seems to be moving backward as you wait and wait. Finally, the veterinarian and his assistant arrived, but all the superhuman efforts proved to be for naught as it became a recovery of a dead foal instead of a live birth. The focus changed to saving the mare only. That is exactly what happened, but the story doesn't end there.

The foal would have been a beautiful black-and-white pinto stud colt. Carmel took the loss as one would expect. After the dead foal was removed from the stall and buried, Carmel cried almost constantly for three days straight and off and on for several more weeks. They had left the foal in the stall with her for a time for her to say her goodbyes, but goodbyes like this are almost impossible to make quickly.

Carmel was still in bad shape as her uterus had been torn in the process, and whether she would made it through the healing process was questionable at best. The whole event weighed heavily on the shoulders of Linda and Jim as they had an important decision to make. It was decided this would be the last year that J-BAR-L Miniatures would breed horses. Did this decision mean Marble was out of a job? Well, not for the current year as she moved from Carmel's stall to Bambi's stall, right on schedule, and stayed until it was time for Bambi's quite normal delivery. After this delivery and one foal delivered for a friend, Marble retired from being a nursemaid and now rules regally over her barn with enough friendship in her heart for all who ask.

Carmel? She became motherly toward another foal born about a week after she lost her foal. She didn't try to nurse the foal but was very protective of it during interaction with other herd mates. Her motherly instinct remained very strong, and now she has a great job helping people experiencing challenges others know little about. She is the consummate therapy horse, and she loves her job.

All things in their own time, all things for their own reason. I, for one, am glad Marble was there for Carmel and, Carmel, in turn for all the other lives she will touch. It is all a circle, unending.

Hope is one of the few things stronger than fear.
Plant seeds of hope and tend your garden well.

Researching this book led me to another of those virtual friendships that regularly occur in this age of social media. Jill Craft of Oregon is another believer in the magical abilities of animals. She experienced one of life's oddities when her German shepherd Avery apparently tried to tell her something was going on in her body, and it needed to be addressed. It was only upon reflection that the message was received and recognized. Although brief, the incident was powerful.

Jill's Eyes

JILL GOT AVERY FROM SOME homeless people who could not take care of his needs. He was a mess when he first arrived at his forever home, with problems that included having a case of mange that wasn't spotted until the other two dogs caught it. Jill held him in her arms a lot when he first came to them. He not only seemed to need the reassurance the connection brought, but he relaxed at her touch. Early in their period of learning about each other, Avery would sniff Jill's eyes quite often. At first, it was a bit disconcerting, but it changed from being strange to being something she looked forward to. He would get close, his eyes would look into hers, and he would repeatedly sniff but never touch her eye or lid. He acted like she had something really great smelling like bacon on her eyelids. He sometimes sniffed her husband's eyes but not as much as he did hers.

Five months after Avery came into their lives, Jill was diagnosed with a viral infection in her right eye and ended up losing the eye. After she returned home from surgery, she picked Avery up, expecting him to once again sniff her eyes. On this particular day, he smelled her eyes often, but it was the look on his face that Jill found curious. It was almost a look of peace that wasn't there before. That was the last day he sniffed at her eyes. It was as if he needed to make sure everything was all right before stopping. Avery never smelled her eyes or her husband's again after he apparently received the validation that Jill was okay. It was all he needed.

Avery has been stuck to Jill's side nonstop over this past year. See, Jill was diagnosed with peritoneal cancer, rated at a stage three. Since the diagnosis, she has never had to wonder where Avery is because he is always close to her side. Jill said, "I get nothing but peace from his presence in my life, and that presence is my lifeline."

And a glimpse through the veil ended up being an introduction to the wondrous world of animal synchronicities and possibly a lifesaving heads-up from their newest family member. Avery has definitely found his forever home.

> It just so happens that I am one of those people who
> consider animals a bit more evolved than we humans
> and know they have much to teach me.
>
> — *Unspoken Messages*

My friendship with Angela Townsend did not begin on the internet but instead through a local writers' group. She and her husband, Steve, live in Elizabethtown, Kentucky, and have become fast friends. Angela is an excellent author and fiction writer with four books published. She also writes short stories. Her husband is a talented photographer. There is no lack of creativity with these two, and I always look forward to her next book and his next picture.

Cody Saves Angela

I N 2015, ANGELA'S HEALTH BEGAN to deteriorate until she barely functioned. Nothing appeared outwardly wrong, but she suffered from an alarming list of symptoms, including joint pain and debilitating fatigue. Her doctor called her the poster child for hypothyroidism and ordered extensive blood tests and an ultrasound of Angela's thyroid, but every test came back normal. Several months later, she broke down and cried in her doctor's office. Angela told her, "Something is *wrong* with me." She begged for help, but without a diagnosis, no help could be given.

Angela and Steve share their home with seven indoor cats, all adopted from animal shelters. I feel the need to give you a little background on Cody. After meeting him and knowing his past, you will find the story even more moving. The year was 2008 when the Townsends decided to get another cat to be company for their year-old rescue, Melody. Well, they came home with two, Cody, also a year-old, and three-year-old Sherman. The three became fast friends in short order. Cody has been what the refuge considered a "throw and go," meaning someone dropped him off during the hours of darkness. The morning after, the volunteers found him walking up the driveway, apparently ready to surrender himself.

Richard D. Rowland

During a veterinarian checkup later, it was discovered that Cody had been shot three times by what was probably a BB gun, and the BBs were still inside him. Welcome to the inhumanity of some humans, Cody. It was decided it would be more traumatic to take them out than just to leave them. Angela said, "They remain a part of Cody to this day, a dark reminder that he somehow escaped death when a person shot him, somehow avoided being killed by a car on a narrow road when a person dumped him, and somehow decided to walk up the graveled driveway to the Refuge Center instead of running away into the woods bordering the road.

"I know in my heart that my God is Cody's God, and I believe He protected and directed this special tiger cat through every danger until Cody arrived at the place where I was meant to find him. Cody is one of the most loving, perceptive cats with whom I've ever been privileged to share my life. And it is because of him that I still have a life to share." Now read on and discover Cody's purpose.

When her health began to decline, Cody, their now-eight-year-old tiger-striped male, began to sleep beside her head on the bed every night. Before long, he shared her pillow. Angela enjoyed falling asleep to his soothing, warm purr, but Cody would pat her face throughout the night, pressing his paws hard against her cheeks and mouth. He would sometimes use the tips of his claws to wake her again and again. She would pet him as he sniffed her nose, and he would purr her to sleep once more. If she nudged him off the bed during the night, his paws would hit the floor like springs, levitating him instantly back onto her pillow. Angela said, "Cody and I share a close bond. I didn't have the heart to shut him out of the room, so I tolerated the interruptions night after night, even when his claws left a small scratch on my bottom lip."

A year later, in an effort to identify the source of her illness, Angela's doctor ordered a sleep study. The study revealed that she suffered from

148

severe obstructive sleep apnea, which caused her to stop breathing thirty to forty times an hour throughout the night. Sleep apnea is common, but it can cause a myriad of health problems. As the vital organs repeatedly labor to function without oxygen night after night, and as the body struggles to wake up so the patient can breathe, the patient is at an ever-increasing risk of suffering a heart attack or stroke—or of not waking up at all.

In addition to prescribing a CPAP machine to ensure she didn't stop breathing while she slept, the doctor discovered a couple of critical vitamin deficiencies had caused her body to mimic hypothyroidism. With supplements and a restored sleep schedule, Angela is recovering fully from the debilitating and frightening symptoms that plagued her for more than two years.

Angela's husband works third shift, so she sleeps alone several nights a week. The first night she used the CPAP machine, she slept four hours straight—the longest stretch of continuous sleep she'd had in more than a year. Cody didn't wake her that night and, since then, has only awakened her on rare occasions. For instance, if she has a cold and tries to sleep without her CPAP, or if she rolls over in such a way that the machine's air flow is inhibited. He's twelve years old now. Angela calls him her Tiger Prince. Alone at night except for Cody, a 12-pound tiger with the heart of a hero, there is no doubt in Angela's mind Cody is the reason she is alive and well today.

Angela reports, "Cody still sleeps beside me on the bed. He purrs me to sleep, and we both enjoy a full night of peace and rest." And two more souls join the ever-growing list of those who believe animals are much more evolved than we have been led to believe.

A life spent in the company of animals
is a life well spent.

Now, to tell the story of Peek-a-boo the blind cat but not before a little background and a cautionary addition that sometimes it isn't about the message but simply about the love. Peeks (as he is affectionately known) was a blind cat who lived in Indiana with his keeper, Dawn Alexander, and her husband John. Peeks was not just challenged by blindness but by a myriad of health-related issues, including hydrocephalus (fluid on the brain), a tumor on his pituitary gland called acromegaly that caused excessive growth, diabetes, and hypertrophic cardiomyopathy (thickening of the heart wall). However, none of that stopped him from having a full life and may have just enhanced his ability to see or feel the things we miss.

Peek-a-Boo, I See Illness

P EEKS CAME TO LIVE WITH Dawn and John in 2005 as a five-month-old kitten. He just showed up in Dawn's yard one day, lost and confused about where home was. He had belonged to a neighbor who had little respect for animals and Peeks was an outside cat. Dawn had seen him in their yard before, but until he visited her, she had no idea he was eyeless. Once Peeks showed up at what was to be his new home, it was just accepted that he now belonged to new keepers.

According to Dawn, "Peeks acted like he owned the place from day one. He had a silly notched tongue that always hung out. He was also a bit of a bully and would swat at my rat terrier's legs and bite his Persian sister's tail. I don't think he ever realized he didn't have eyes, for he sat at doors and windows 'looking' outside as if he could see perfectly. He ran around the house at full speed, recklessly knocking into furniture. To watch Peeks move about his day, you'd never know he was blind or tested by other medical issues."

Peeks was not described as a sweet, loving cat by any means. He was described as a bully actually. He would bully Dawn's rat terrier and her Persian, Mai Tai. She knew he cared for her in his own way because he was always near, content with them just being in the same room. He was, however, extremely receptive to human emotions. If Dawn cried, he would run over to her and almost cling to her side. It's as if he wanted to offer comfort to her.

When Dawn's senior Persian cat started having serious health problems, she thought she would need to figure out a way to keep them separated because Peeks always started trouble. He didn't want to fight, but he sure did enjoy his rough play. Mai Tai didn't enjoy roughhousing when she was well, so she certainly didn't want any part of it when sick. It turned out Dawn didn't have to do anything because he started leaving her alone on his own. He even began cuddling up to her on a regular basis, apparently for both comfort and as a naptime buddy. Peeks had never acted like that toward her in the past. Did he know she was ill? I think the answer to that would be a resounding yes. His ability to note physical changes and challenges in other beings became obvious after a few years of observation.

As noted earlier, Peeks was somewhat of a standoffish bully, but there were times his softer side came out and took over. That was the case with Dawn's mother, Jill. Even though we have never met in person, Jill and I share the same diagnosis and life challenge. What Jill learned from Peeks came after reflection on the last three years of his life. Peeks had always treated Jill the same way he treated everyone. But then Peeks became increasingly clingy with Jill the last three years of his life. Starting around 2013, or three years before Jill was diagnosed, he would sit by her feet and rub around her legs to the point of annoying her. While he was always very nosy and enjoyed being near, he was *not* at all affectionate with anyone else but her. This new side of Peeks continued for the rest of his life.

One of the things about multiple myeloma is it can lie in a smoldering state for years before rearing its ugly head and becoming symptomatic.

Did Peeks know something was coming and offer his reassurance that all would be okay? I know what I believe and live in hopes you can see the patterns in the lives of the animals sharing time with us.

Peeks adapted to his challenges well. Was it because he had never known anything different and just adapted to what he had? In spite of or maybe because of his challenges, I think quite possibly Peeks was also given a great gift. He had the ability to sense something was amiss with Jill and offered the one thing he had much of: love.

Peeks took a bad turn in 2014 when his own health took a downturn. It started innocently enough with an increase in intake of both water and food and led to an eventual diagnosis of acromegaly (a tumor on the pituitary gland) that causes excess growth and other negative factors. On April 13, 2016, Peeks was euthanized after experiencing a bowel blockage, but only after all alternatives were discussed. It was simply his time.

Peek-a-Boo left many memories that make you either smile or tear up while thinking about the depth of soul this cat possessed. I believe he knew of the trials Jill would be facing, and furthermore, he knew he wouldn't be there when she found out what was in front of her. What he did was share both love and a sense of peace with Jill as long as he drew breath. His lesson? That out of all the emotions someone diagnosed with cancer feels, perhaps love and peace are the most important to focus upon. Travel on, Mr. Peeks. Although blind, your soul sight was powerful and much appreciated.

No one is too old for fairy tales or magic.

On February 28, 1994, life changed for Lyne Paulson. She was visiting a friend in Florida and was involved in a vehicle accident that left her with many challenges, most notably, amnesia, a severed artery, a concussion, loss of short-term memory, and a broken cheekbone. Challenged? I'd say without doubt. The good news is Doctor Abby was on the case. Abby is Lyne's cat, and she had a good plan of treatment for Lyne's ills.

Doctor Abby

A s LYNE TELLS IT, "FROM the first night back home from the hospital, Abby became my shadow, following me everywhere. If we had to go anywhere, she sat looking out the living room window waiting for us. Upon our return, she would run to the back door so she could greet me and inspect me for any problems. If she found nothing new, she would run to the couch so she could be there if I decided to sit down. If I were too tired for the couch, she would follow me to the bedroom, jump up on the bed, and wait for me to lie down."

If Lyne sat on the couch, Abby would drape herself around her neck and begin purring in her ear, always placing her head on the injured side of Lyne's head where the vibrations of her purr could be felt the most. If she were lying on the bed, Abby would ignore her instincts to face the door and drape herself so Lyne could feel that healing purr.

The first month Lyne was home, she had to have someone drive her everywhere she went. Her optic nerve had been shaken badly, and she had double vision that limited her navigation. Lyne felt Abby knew this too, as she would direct her everywhere she went. Her little body would touch her ankle, and she told her through her meows where Abby thought she should be. She also knew Lyne couldn't tolerate loud voices and yelling. If the kids were playing and getting too loud, she would run up to one of them and put her paw over the offender's mouth.

For the entire six months Lyne was in therapy, Abby was her shadow. The day Lyne was released from therapy, Abby stopped being her shadow, although at naptime and bedtime, she continued to drape herself across the top of Lyne's head, especially if she started getting a migraine. Abby could tell when the migraines were coming on better than Lyne could.

Abby was nineteen when she passed away. Lyne can still feel her and hear her when she gets a migraine. Lyne said, "I miss one of the best doctors I ever had, but I can still feel her energy around me. Even though she may be physically gone, spiritually, she never left."

Lyne was open to the magic that surrounds us through the lives of animals before the accident happened, which may have made her experience with Abby easier to accept as a perfect example of a glimpse behind the veil. Abby knew something was different when Lyne returned home, and she went right to work, healing and bringing relief to her keeper.

Once and a while something amazing comes
along that makes you question
all you ever knew.
May today be your day.

Rather than animals helping humans, this story deals with animals helping other animals through a challenge. Pam Cox of South Carolina shared time with two horses and described them as "entirely different geldings" that existed at opposite ends of the spectrum from each other. Dakota, a red chestnut saddlebred, is a comic and very extroverted. He loves people and the interaction he has with them. Her other horse, named Ranger, is a chestnut blanket Appaloosa. He is very introverted but is also a tough guy. Pam said, "Some would say Ranger was perpetually grumpy." He was retired from teaching jumping due to arthritis.

Dakota and Ranger

P AM GOT HER START MUCH like the rest of us. It would have been nice to have inherited a farm, but Pam, like many of us, had to wait until the time was right to stake a claim on her own place. After many years of want, this is exactly what happened.

Dakota and Ranger had their own small shed row barn in the pasture and most of the day were free to go in or stay out at their comfort. The only time they were shut in their stalls was at feeding time. It made things easier rather than watching the inevitable battle over food when horses compete. Pam found it odd that before coming to this farm, Dakota was usually at the bottom of the pecking order, while Ranger was usually alpha. Even after getting used to each other, the dominance standing stayed as it was. It seemed as if they tolerated each other and lived in the same space. Dakota would boss Ranger around, and Ranger would comply. There was little mutual grooming or fond interactions between the two of them.

Pam told me during the first or possibly second winter at their farm, they had a "once every few years snowstorm." When they do get snow in the Piedmont area of South Carolina, it is not odd to get sleet on top of it, and that is what happened this time. Pam had blanketed the horses earlier because of the extremely low wind chill. While the snow was flying, Pam fed them their afternoon ration inside, and everything was well even though the storm left seven inches of snow on the ground. An unusually large amount of snow for the area was being followed by sleet once again. Pam knew she would have to check on the horses before retiring for the night.

At ten o'clock that night, Pam went back outside to check on the horses one last time, and what she saw was both amazing and concerning. Pam said, "What I found was Dakota standing against the side of the barn where there was no protection from the sleet. He was pawing the ground vigorously, and his distress was very apparent. Colic was my first thought. But there on Dakota's side that was away from the barn (facing the sleet) was Ranger. Ranger was taking the sleet for his herd mate. Ranger's neck, face, ears and legs were covered in ice, as was his blanket. He was trying his best to protect Dakota. Ranger's blanket had so much ice that when I finally got it off, it stood by itself in the tack room. Thankfully, I had a spare."

Ranger was not only blocking the ill weather from reaching Dakota, but he was also protecting Dakota. As Dakota was wanting to pace and was acting like he wanted to roll, Ranger's calming presence kept those things from happening. Ranger was there, head down and showing a palpable peace that spread to Dakota. His pawing of the ground was the only sign of discomfort, which was unusual for him with colic.

After getting the horses inside and changing their blankets, Pam took vitals on Dakota and called the veterinarian. Her worry about colic was valid. Dakota had a case of colic along with a systemic infection that caused a high fever from a virus. She nursed Dakota through his illness for a few days, and he recovered completely. It seemed to Pam she lived in the barn for three days with the phone to her ear talking to the veterinarian. The vet talked Pam through the treatment protocol because she could not get to the farm due to the weather. Apparently, Pam was a quick study. All turned out well when the vet was finally able to come.

Dakota not only recovered; he changed. Both horses changed. Pam said, "There was a distinct change in the dynamics between the two. They became fast friends, often found grooming each other." The image of crusty old Ranger protecting his friend is one that will stay with Pam forever. She was blessed to witness a change. Dakota took a step back, and when he stepped forward again, he did so with a brand-new, lifelong friend.

Change never fails to amaze me. Here you are going through life, and you think you are comfortable with things just as they are. It matters not how good or bad things are; there is a comfort in the sameness of the day. Then, seemingly out of nowhere, the universe challenges you, and you find that you have to accept the challenge or it will be forced upon you. Speaking as one who has been challenged in a major way, it is at this point in life when you have to step back and do some reflecting about all you have been taught and told about this life we live. Maybe, just maybe, those who taught us really didn't know the answers after all.

Once you embrace the change, life really does go through a much-needed metamorphosis. A lightness replaces the weight that you didn't even realize you were carrying, as if some miracle diet worked to truly rid you of unwanted pounds. Anger, disappointment, sadness, uncertainty, and more all fall to the side like winter leaves in the wind, and a new you will emerge—a new you who has learned the lesson offered and hungers for more.

> Remember, change is constant, lessons are
> abundant and in the end, all will be good.
>
> — *Unspoken Messages*

The good thing about the internet and social media is the reach your words and ideas may have. That is exactly what happened when I posted a request for people to share their animal stories with me for this book. I was contacted by Ana, who, with her husband, Maxim, lives in the Eastern Plains area of Russia, outside a small scenic town called Rostov. Fortunately, her English is good because, sadly, my Russian is sorely lacking and limited to a few phrases. She had a story to tell, and quite frankly, it intrigued me enough to write her back with more questions. What developed is another of those virtual friendships that you hope culminates in a someday face-to-face meeting. I'd love to meet them both!

A Dream Horse

WHAT HAPPENS TO A LIFELONG equine enthusiast when she reaches middle age? Well, that person might start looking for that one project horse—one she would get as a weanling. She would plan to raise it, train it herself, and have a longtime partner to journey forth with and explore the world. Those were the thoughts Ana had been having of late. She had this dream of a white stallion with chiseled features—one of those horses people stare at with mouths agape and ask a thousand questions about just so they can remain in its presence. She even had a name picked out to gift the horse when she found it. She knew that not just any horse would work; this one was going to be special. Little did she know the universe had other plans for her and the horse she wanted so badly. She would soon find out the universe was more about personal growth and less about filling a grocery list checkoff order.

The horse Ana ended up with did not come to her as a foal or weanling, but she did meet the horse shortly after it was born. She was at another farm taking a look at a foal for a friend of hers when she spied a little foal that she instantly felt sorry for. In her words, she had this to say about the initial meeting: "She was a runt of a filly that looked like she was created by using spare and mismatched parts. She simply did not look like she was put together right. She was born after a very difficult delivery and one that she probably shouldn't have survived. The first time I saw her, her mother kicked her into oblivion right in front of me. She did a few somersaults but kept going on those crooked little legs without fail. I remember thinking that must have surely left a mark."

Before leaving, she wished the foal a good life and never gave the horse a second thought. Then, four years later, the same breeder called, apparently in distress. They had sold the horse as a three-year-old, and it was going to be put in a professional training program to become a show horse. Her possible career ended when they discovered she just wasn't a trainable or a trustworthy horse. She was subject to blowups that seemingly came from nowhere. They were making plans to sell her at auction where she would be slaughtered and sold as meat. The horse slaughter business is brisk in Russia. The breeder did not want to see it happen but never asked Ana to take the horse—well, not out loud anyway.

Normally, Ana would have wished the horse well and gone on with her life. However, something felt off about the whole experience, and without telling anyone her thoughts, she decided to sleep on the possibility of taking this horse on as a project.

That very night as they slept, Ana's nonhorsey husband, Maxim, woke her up to tell her about a dream he'd just had. He told her someone or some power had spoken to him in a dream and told him the name of the bay horse to come was Kpacota. At the time, he had no idea another horse was coming or Ana's thoughts about taking that particular horse. He returned to sleep and left Ana to her thoughts. Of course, she knew what *Kpacota* meant. It meant beauty, as well as loveliness, good looks, glory, and goodliness. And it was decided right then that she would adopt the horse and would call her Cota. The sign came, and the sign was accepted.

The next morning, she called the breeder and said she would take the bay filly sight unseen—period. Ana's plan was to take the filly for six months, finish her, and get her to a good forever home. Then she would continue her search for her white stallion. Well, that first six months turned into six more and six more until she reached a point where she felt like she was participating in "an epic foster failure." She just couldn't seem to make any headway, and Cota's future was dimming.

After one exceptionally rough ride, Ana had to attempt an emergency dismount, and her foot stuck in the stirrup. She described it as seeing her life flash before her eyes as she desperately hung between the saddle and the ground, screaming in pain. Cota stopped in her tracks and never moved other than to look back at her charge. After untangling herself from the stirrup, she hit the ground and sat there a moment, sobbing. With Cota gently grazing close to her, she asked herself why she was doing this. It was impossible! And then she looked to the ground while her mind searched for answers. While her mind was busy in thought, her eyes saw a four-leaf clover. Yes, they are as rare in Russia as they are here. Then she saw another and another and another. In the end, she found seventeen four-leaf clovers.

Being someone who tends to lean toward the spiritual side of life as we know it, Ana did a search for the importance of the number seventeen. What she found was seventeen is an indication you are on the right path in your life. "Seventeen is a very promising sign that your current life path is leading you to manifest good fortune," she explained. "Your angels are always looking out for you, providing messages of encouragement and inspiration." You do not have to be incredibly insightful to see the sign sent.

I asked Ana if anything changed after discovering the seventeen clovers in the pasture, and she answered with a resounding *yes*. She added, "An older gentleman told me soon after I got Cota and was limping around at the feed store after a good fall that an alpha mare needs a full year to think and digest before they accept you and call you their own. My initial reaction was doubtful. I thought that he just wanted to comfort me and give me hope. Lord behold, he knew what he was talking about. After a year, she totally turned around. She is a new horse. She even looks different; people do not recognize her. Cota is always going to be a firecracker and will have her mare moments, so she will not be a family horse. She is truly a one-person horse, and I am her person. She fiercely protects me like her prized possession. She would go through fire for me, perhaps not literally but very close."

Ana said she was very happy with the choices the universe made for her. Cota is her personal, once-in-a-lifetime horse and is where she will stay forever. Will there ever be a white stallion in Ana's life? Never say never, but for now, life is perfect. Spasibo (thank you) for sharing your story with us, Ana.

Things change. It has always been that way.

Continuing the theme of messages received subliminally or via communication, here is a story that had its origins in New York City. Meet Jane Davis of Woodstock, New York. She and her dog Dreidel had an experience, and I am grateful she decided to share it with us.

Messages from Dreidel

AT TEN O'CLOCK ONE SUNNY but crisp October morning, Jane was at work on the eighteenth floor of the Helmsley building, which overlooks Park Avenue in New York. She was suddenly and unexpectedly awash with dread. The dread came with an intuitive feeling that something was horribly wrong with her dog Dreidel who was home alone. Jane trusted the feeling and quickly announced that she had to go home. She practically ran the fifteen blocks to her apartment.

Jane said, "When I got inside, Dreidel was sitting there as if waiting for me and was breathing deeply—breathing in a very strained and unusual manner. I quickly called her vet and asked, 'Can I put the speakerphone on so you can hear her?' After listening for a minute, there was a moment of silence that hung in the air. 'Can you bring her in?' the doctor asked. At that moment, I knew. 'Yes,' I said weakly. I intuitively knew what he meant."

Dreidel was Jane's special lifetime dog and had been with her eighteen years. When she first got her, she had a dog-naming party. Fifteen people sat in a circle with a small puppy in the middle. The pup leapt up and started chasing her tail. Someone shouted that she looked like a dreidel, which would roughly translate to a spinning top. The party was over, and the name decided. Dreidel was a mixed breed dog of unknown origin. She had a long beige coat and beautiful, expressive eyes. The connection between Jane and Dreidel was as old as time itself.

Back in the apartment, while Jane was hugging and petting her, Dreidel sat straight up, put a paw on Jane's arm, and looked her in the eye. Jane said it was as if she were saying, "Let's go, Mom. It's time. I'm okay." She hugged Dreidel tightly and hailed a taxi, cradling her during the entire trip.

They arrived at the veterinarian's office, and after the examination, Jane received the news she had been fearing. It was time for Dreidel to cross over. She was old, and her lungs had filled with fluid. She was in extreme distress, and nothing could be done to correct the issue. It was simply time. Jane said, "Saying goodbye was excruciating. She looked in my eyes as if comforting me while she drifted off." And then the tears flowed freely and still do when remembering this special animal.

Two months after Dreidel's passing, Jane had Dreidel's urn in her hands as she walked around. After a short visit with her beloved pet, Jane put the urn back in its cabinet, and as she did, she received an unmistakable message saying, "Not yet please." Thinking it odd but nothing more, she ignored the message and returned the urn to its shelf.

Talking on the phone with her sister Nancy a short time later, both of them heard a loud crash. Nancy asked what it was. Jane replied that she didn't know, but it almost sounded as if a mirror had shattered. After checking, Jane couldn't find anything broken, so she sat down on her couch to continue her conversation. As she sat, she was looking through the glass of a large hutch that held china and pottery. The hutch was also the resting place for Dreidel's ashes. Jane noticed the top of the tin urn was not on the base where it belonged.

Thinking it odd, Jane got up to examine the urn and saw that the top was on the other side of the shelf from the urn, and some of the china had been broken from the force of the urn and top separating.

She took the urn back out of the hutch and decided she needed to pay attention to the message she had received earlier. Jane said, "And I sat. Still. Holding Dreidel. Listening. Remembering that there is a whole world of language around us if only we take the time to hear."

I am grateful to Jane for sharing this story of life, loss, discovery, magic, synchronicity, and love. She knows firsthand what many of us only surmise. She has seen what few see, and she is at peace. I think that is a perfect place to be. She made Dreidel a promise that day to get her out of the hutch on a regular basis and for longer periods of time in order to have proper visits. The urn has stayed intact ever since. No one knows better than Dreidel when it is time to go out.

> How am I to know how far I can travel
> if I never take a step?

There is a possibility I could have written a complete book about subliminal messages sent from animals to humans. Maybe you will read these words and think of the synchronicities that have happened in your life that changed the focus of your day. Changing focus sure seems to have been the case with Polly Hershey of Flower Mound, Texas, who had to do just that on a rainy day while on her way to work.

The Right Right Turn

LIKE MOST OF US, POLLY is a creature of habit. She goes to work the same way day after day and month after month. It is her daily ritual—well, until one particular day, anyway. On that day, she missed the turn she had made forever. She turned right at the next road, intending to make another right and get back on her route. It was raining so hard that even with the windshield wipers on full speed, she could barely see where she was going. She came to a place where water was rushing across the pavement and had to come to a complete stop. It was then she saw something large and dark emerge from the water and haltingly make its way to the nearby lawn of a condo complex.

Polly ignored the pouring rain and left her car to investigate. And this is where the synchronicities become amazing. What Polly found was a huge snapping turtle. His shell was cracked and his jaw was broken on both sides. Apparently, he had been run over and left for dead.

Let's let Polly explain the first thought that came to her as she studied this dilemma. "It immediately struck me that a new vet place had just opened directly across the street. I jumped in my car and zoomed over there. Drenching wet, I ran in and explained I needed a big box for this huge turtle. About that time, the new vet came from the back and said he would go with me to help. I couldn't believe my luck!

165

What a hero! Off we went to rescue our new friend. Mr. Snapper tried lunging, which was a little scary for him and us. I had recently been in real estate and remembered I had a stack of metal name riders in my trunk. I retrieved those, and because there were about four of them, they were pretty sturdy when all held together. The fit under his shell between front and back legs was perfect. We gently slid the metal up under him and slowly placed him in the box. He didn't try to fight us."

Polly explained that the doctor gave the turtle a shot to help him deal with the shock his body was experiencing and then weighed him. He weighed in at a whopping twenty-five pounds—a very big boy who was probably around twenty years old. They put the turtle in a dog run, and Polly went to work knowing two things: one, they would understand her being late after they heard her story and saw the condition of her attire, and two, she had to find someone to rehab the turtle. At the time, there weren't a lot of people who could take on such a project.

Then it came to her in a flash. Just two days before, she had seen a public service announcement (PSA) on a local channel about a rescue center just south of the Dallas area. Polly had never seen the PSA before and hasn't seen it since. She called the center and explained what had happened and what she was looking for. Interestingly enough, the woman on the phone had worked at a zoo for many years in the reptile/amphibian area and, like Polly, was a huge turtle lover. After talking a bit and reaching an agreement for care and rehab, Polly made arrangements to deliver the turtle the next morning. The lady who ran the rehab facility was named Karen, and she said she had the perfect veterinarian to treat this new charge. His shell would be repaired and his jaw wired shut, leaving just enough room to tube feed him during the recovery phase. The turtle lived in Karen's dining room both prior to and after the surgery and was tube fed baby food daily.

Karen told Polly that the turtle was the gentlest and sweetest snapper she had ever encountered. After his wires were removed, Karen would feed him raw chicken on the bone. He would gently take it from her hand and then devour it with gusto. He knew who was helping him and respected her for what she was doing. After the turtle recovered enough to return to the wild, he went to live out his days on a large ranch with several ponds and few roads.

The synchronicities in this story are many. Polly said, "The interesting series of events of the turtle rescue to this day give me goose bumps. First, I missed a turn I had never missed. Why? To find this turtle. Second, I quickly recalled the vet who had just opened across the street, and he came to the rescue. Third, I had seen a PSA two days before when I should have been asleep and never saw it again—kind of weird. Fourth, the rehabber had so much experience with all types of turtles. Fifth, that turtle never struck out at anybody handling him. I know he knew he was being helped by many people."

As far as we know, the turtle lived and may still be living a nice life in his new home, all thanks to a missed turn and the universe lining things up with all the help he needed to recover. Keep in mind the universe did most of those things before that rainy day in Texas. Curious, isn't it?

This was not the only experience Polly has had with synchronicity and turtles. I am one to believe once the universe finds people with open minds to its enchanted ways, it sends even more to you. Polly possessed an open mind, a kind heart, and a deep affection for the animal kingdom, especially chickens and turtles.

As the story goes, she was working late one day catching up on things because she had been late that morning due to a doctor's appointment. When she arrived that morning, she was unable to park in her regular spot and had to park in a different area close to some cardboard awaiting recycling. As she walked to her car at the end of the day, something caught her eye. She saw a turtle walking at a very fast pace in a southerly direction toward a road. She ran back to the recycling section and retrieved a big box, raced back to the turtle, and scooped him up. At first, she though it was a box turtle, but upon reflection, something was different about him. His feet were huge and the legs reminded her of elephant legs. Neither of those had slowed him down, and he motored quite quickly when compared to other Texas turtles. Polly was quite sure she had never seen a turtle like this one.

She took her new charge to her home where she cut up some juicy cantaloupe for him. He ate with gusto, as if starving and possibly very thirsty. He ate so fast the juice flowed from the corner of his mouth and even his nostrils. After the cantaloupe was gone, she cut him up some cucumber, and he ate all that too.

She called a neighbor who had horses to inquire if he had a trough she could use for a few days. He did and delivered it. This same neighbor informed Polly he was a tortoise, not a turtle. Her first thought was that they do not have tortoises in north Texas—well, until now they didn't. Polly made a temporary home for the turtle in the trough, complete with sandy soil, small oak limbs with leaves for shade, and a hidey hole when he wanted privacy. He ate some more that night and drank his fill of fresh water before retiring.

Then began a three times a day feeding schedule split between Polly and her husband. Polly remembered thinking the first night that he had died. She checked on him, and he was lying in the tub with all four legs spread out, his neck straight out, and his eyes closed. She looked closely and could see he was just sleeping deeply. This was one tired fella. The next morning, he was released in the yard for a short walkabout while breakfast was being fixed. He looked well rested and even perky. After putting him back in the tub, she moved everything into the garage for the day.

She and her husband bought and installed some temporary sixteen-inch fencing and built him an enclosure, complete with shade and concealment. Then, they began their search to find out what he was. Polly was in a pet supply store one day and picked up a little book about turtles and tortoises. And right there in the book was a one-inch picture of him, without a doubt. He was a Texas tortoise. They are from the southern Texas area and live in desertlike conditions. They are also an endangered species. Their main diet is prickly pear cactus, so Polly immediately stocked up on some for him in addition to keeping his favorite veggies on hand. Polly fed him by hand, and he became very gentle with her, eating close to her fingers but never once biting her.

After a couple of weeks of the routine, she would see him rear up on two legs and lean on the enclosure fence with his head sticking over as she pulled in the driveway. There he was, waiting on her. Oh, the tortoise also had a name now. He was Ziggy because of his gait being one of zigging and zagging as he walked.

Polly knew she had to find the proper home for him, and the search for one began. By this time, Ziggy had been with them for almost eight weeks. After eating in the afternoon, Polly would pick him up in her lap, and he would crawl up and rest his head on her shoulder with his face against her neck and sleep his afternoon nap. As the search continued, Polly found a reptile rescue group south of Dallas. They did not house turtles or tortoises, but they knew someone who did. They recommended the San Angelo Nature Center, which happened to be in Ziggy's native territory. She called and spoke to them, and they said they had room for Ziggy. Arrangements were made for a relay of Ziggy from Polly to his new home.

I best turn this part over to Polly: "When the sad day came to turn him over, my husband and son held him and loved on him one last time. It makes me tear up just writing this. I tucked him into a cozy picnic basket and made the hour or so drive to meet the folks taking Ziggy on the next leg of the journey. They headed to Austin with my little charge. It was so difficult to let him go, but I wanted the best and safest home for him and certainly found it.

"I called the following Monday to be sure they had arrived safely back in San Angelo, and they had. The next week, I called again to check on him. The curator had small kids, and by this time, school had started back up. He told me his kids' teacher always called and asked him to bring an animal based on the letter they were studying. And guess what? Yep, they were working on the letter *T*, so Ziggy went to school. The curator said the kids just loved him, and Ziggy let them gently rub his head and neck, just like we had done."

Polly will never know how Ziggy got from south Texas to north Texas where she saved him, but she was curious about his direction of travel every time he was released for a walkabout. He always traveled in a southerly direction. She was told he was simply trying to get home. Tortoises' internal navigation systems keep them moving south toward home until they either reach home or die from a lack of food, water, or road accident. Without Polly's intervention, the odds were Ziggy would have died trying to get home. I am reminded of a quote by Ram Dass that goes like this: "We are all just walking each other home." That we are. What some do not realize is this includes every living being on this rock, not just us humans.

Polly said, "The day I found him was a special day for my family. The scenario of why I was there at that specific time and parked in that specific spot was not a coincidence. I truly believe God has always put me in places where an animal needs help, and this was just one more of those times. Had I not had a doctor's appointment, I wouldn't have been parked outside at the farthest corner, and I wouldn't have been working late. I started to leave the office at six o'clock but saw something else I needed to work on, so stayed until seven o'clock. Again, not a coincidence. And it wasn't an accident I found the wonderful home for him in the safety of the wildlife center where nobody could snatch him up again and carry him away! We talk about Ziggy from time to time. He was a special little guy, and I feel very blessed to have been his foster mom."

I feel blessed Polly shared those two stories with us. I will let them stand as proof that all animals need our love, protection, and care. Sometimes we need to be comfortable intervening in order to save them, and other times we need to learn to leave them alone and let nature do what it does best. All creatures need to be able to feel comfortable in our presence and know that we are here to help, not harm them.

> There is a certain nobility in compassion and a beauty
> in the empathy that accompanies it.
> Live your life in such a way that other beings may live
> a better one because of your actions.

Do animals have a way of stimulating your intuition as a means of communicating with you? I not only think it is possible, but I believe it is undoubtedly true. Those little feelings you get that seem to come from nowhere are actually communications from away, and those messages can be powerfully demanding of your attention.

This next story was relayed to me by Laurel of Edmonton, Alberta, Canada, who at the time lived with her parents at Canadian Forces Base Cold Lake. Her father was a career member of the Canadian Air Force.

The road to coexisting with animals, especially dogs, was full of stops, starts, fear, and sometimes sheer terror before finally arriving at a place of love for Laurel—a place where she would spend the rest of her life in the company of animals.

Loving Lady

L AUREL TOLD ME ABOUT THE beginning of her life with animals. Initially, it was fraught with fear and uncertainty. She went on to relay an incident that described her early feelings completely. She said, "The residential area of Cold Lake had no fenced yards, and it was common for people to let their dogs out unaccompanied, and sometimes small packs formed. My earliest memories of dogs bring feelings of sheer terror. I would be paralyzed by fear when I saw any dog. I remember one winter day in grade one when I was walking home for lunch. The grade-one kids got out a half hour earlier than the others, so I wasn't able to wait for my siblings. As I walked, a dog came along, and I started crying. When I stopped, the dog stopped; when I walked, it walked ahead. Again, when I stopped, it stopped and looked at me. When I knew I was close enough to home, I ran as fast as I could and ditched the dog. Looking back now, I wonder if it was trying to protect me."

As Laurel got a little older, she had what she described as a "doggie revival." The couple next door to her acquired a little puppy that looked like a blonde Labrador. It was tied out by the back step, and she would see it every day as she made her way home. This pup wasn't the kind to jump up and down excitedly but instead would roll over onto its back as Laurel approached. It took her a while to get the message, but eventually, she approached the pup and petted its stomach.

Laurel said, "I was hooked. I had never felt anything so soft and beautiful. One day it gave me a great big slurp across the lips, and I flew into the house to wash my face. (Wow, has that changed!) From then on, I begged my parents for a dog."

When her father retired a year later, her parents stood true to their word. Laurel had spent that year studying different breeds of dogs so she could make an educated choice for her first dog. She wanted either a sheltie or a Boston terrier. Her mother chose a beagle, and a beagle it was—a pretty little purebred beagle who became Lady. Lady arrived for Laurel's tenth birthday and was the best gift she ever remembered. At the same time, Laurel's father purchased twenty acres of uncleared land about twenty miles outside Edmonton. He and his brother would travel to the property on weekends to clear land, and they would often take Lady on these weekend trips with them.

Around the time Laurel turned twelve, her interest had shifted away from Lady and toward friends and schoolmates. She remembers quite vividly the morning when her intuition matured. Her father was on his way to the property and intended to take Lady with him. Laurel was awash with anxiety, but the reason was lost to her. She couldn't put her finger on it, but she just knew that something bad was going to happen to Lady if she went with her father. She begged her father not to take Lady with him, but he was steadfast in his decision to take her. No manner of begging would sway him; his mind was made up.

Several times during the day, Laurel was stricken by "gut-wrenching" anxiety about her dog. When she knew it was time for her father to be home, she rushed to check on her dog. Laurel said, "I remember bursting through the door and asking my mom where Lady was. To my great relief, Mom said that Lady was out in the yard. As I charged out the door to see her, Mom yelled that I had to be gentle because Lady had been hit by a car!"

All of a sudden, she knew the reason for her feelings of dread. Luckily, the driver of the vehicle had seen Lady in time to slow down, so only her toes had been "mildly" run over. Some power tried to tell her something was going to happen, and her young mind was not ready to process the message. However, seeds had been planted that would ensure she would be able to receive and understand such messages in the future. Lady recovered with no lasting ill effects except for a limp that lasted only a few days and a newfound respect for vehicles.

This was not the only message that Laurel received from Lady, who passed away at the age of nine. Laurel had graduated from high school by this time and had entered the workforce. Unfortunately, Lady's death was hastened by treatment she was getting for a skin condition. The monthly shots of steroids ended up causing liver failure and her early crossing of the bridge. Laurel said, "I had never experienced the death of anyone close before, and I was devastated. I was a total basket case. I couldn't function at work. When anyone spoke to me, I would burst into tears. I was depressed, and I missed my girl terribly."

Then, true to its nature and just when it was needed the most, the universe provided clarity. Three weeks after Lady's passing, she visited Laurel in a dream, but this wasn't just any old dream. This one felt like reality. It was a dream in which Laurel could feel the warmth of her old friend. In the dream, Laurel and Lady embraced and Laurel said, "Lady, please don't go," to which Lady replied, "I have to go, but remember, I will always love you."

When Laurel awoke, she was convinced that she had actually been in the presence of magic, and the meeting had been real and not a dream. She said, "The feeling was more real than anything I have ever known." She has not forgotten the feeling these many years later. They have become part of who she is and what she believes.

Life is learning to dance with
a broken heart.

On the heels of losing her son of twenty-nine years to an automobile accident, Cathy Minnich of Otis, Oregon, experienced a deep and moving connection with a black-and-white horse that opened her eyes to the magic of the universe and the animal kingdom. Read on and see how animals have the ability to not only recognize the pain and darkness existing within us but also the ability to heal those hurts. The incident she relayed occurred at her sister's farm in Fall City, Oregon, where the horse still lives to this day.

Comet's Magic

IN 2005 CATHY WAS FACED with making a decision to end the life support keeping her twenty-nine-year-old son alive. He had suffered severe injuries in a car accident. The pain involved in making such a decision is something none of us should have to go through, and I am sure her pain resonates with everyone reading these words.

Cathy's sister, recognizing the unacknowledged pain Cathy existed with, invited her out to her farm. When she arrived at the farm, she noticed several horses way off in the distance across a field. Cathy got out of the car and walked over to the gate and just stood there, gazing upon the horses and soaking in the peace provided by her sister.

Cathy said, "Suddenly, a black-and-white paint horse darted across the field, running faster and faster, heading in my direction. For some unknown reason, I knew he knew something was wrong. I felt it, and the feeling kept getting stronger and stronger the closer he came. When he arrived at the gate, he threw his head upon my shoulder. He whispered and nudged me he as he wrapped his head around mine. I never felt so much love, caring, and compassion radiate from another being. The tears flowed as we shared this experience together. He actually whimpered with me in cadence. I will never forget the bond that was forged that day."

The horse's name is Comet, and he is still part of her life. He lives about forty-five minutes from her. Even though their visits have become more sporadic, Cathy said, "I will always call him my special horse, and I will always love him as if he were my own."

Cathy went on to have even more magical interactions with animals such as deer, elk, salmon, eagles, hawks, and bears, and she believes all animals have messages for us, especially if they appear to us more than once. Her most recent encounter was with a mouse. It reminded her of the smaller things in life and not just the proverbial bigger picture. The elk reminded her if we work together in this life, we will remain strong and resilient and reach our goals and destinations. It is when we are divided or do not recognize the lessons that we fail to succeed. However, never worry; lessons are always repeated until we do get them.

Division is indeed a weakness and failure, and if we focus on a way to work together, much more will be accomplished. This black-and-white paint horse exhibited perfect timing and an understanding of the depth of pain being experienced by Cathy. Do you possibly see yourself in this story? Maybe minus the connection with a special being, one full of healing energy. If so, put yourself in the environment, and open your heart to receiving what the universe wants you to possess. You will discover a power you might not know existed.

The moment you let go of the past
is the moment you begin to rise higher.

Bethany Thomas of Canton, Georgia, had quite a tale to tell about animal connections. She was blessed to make the acquaintance of a saddlebred stud named Copper. Read on for her magical encounter.

Copper

IN AUGUST 2013, THE COUNTY animal shelter where Bethany volunteered found itself needing to rescue an entire herd of saddlebreds. Included in this herd were several pregnant mares, emaciated foals, geldings, and one stallion. Because the shelter was only equipped for dogs and cats, they had to find some trustworthy horse farms and rescues to help them. Within a few days, they found wonderful foster homes for the horses, and they were able to find a perfect place for the stallion.

With the help of the Georgia Equine Rescue League, they made him a temporary shelter of his own to protect him from the elements. Later, they built a more suitable, permanent barn. From September to January, he had the whole pasture to himself. And he slowly learned to trust the handful of caregivers who were honored with his care. Bethany was the only volunteer outside of the regular shelter employees, and she referred to it as "the most priceless experience of my life."

Bethany said, "We named him Copper because he shined like a new penny in the sun! The vet said he was approximately six years old. He was not quite as emaciated as the mares and foals because he was still bringing in stud fees for his neglectful owner, but he was still severely underweight."

When Copper arrived, he was terrified of people. It broke their hearts because they wanted so badly to love on him and let him know that everything was going to be okay. Instead, it seemed like he insisted they show him and earn his trust one day, one meal, and one positive experience at a time. Due to his condition, the food had to come slowly and carefully. Some things cannot be rushed, and reintroducing food was one of them.

Bethany said, "Under constant vet care and advisement, we slowly increased his groceries and even more slowly watched as the walls of doubt and distrust began to fall. I am a science teacher who has loved horses my entire life but never owned one. Working with Copper was the first and only time I had the opportunity and privilege to care for a horse on a daily basis. I had the afternoon shift, and I could not wait for the school day to end so I could race to the shelter to see Copper, feed him, groom him, and work on gaining his trust."

Every experience was a first for both of them. Bethany had never had a reason to buy horse treats, brushes, halters, or lead ropes, but then, suddenly, she did! After a month or so, Copper became comfortable with her and she with him. Bethany's Dad was always concerned about his inexperienced daughter going to take care of a stallion … *alone*. But even though she was always alert to danger, Bethany was never afraid in his presence. Copper was never pushy, even though he was starved. He walked slowly behind her as they made their way to his feed bucket, and he would back up just far enough to let her pour the feed into the bucket.

Bethany touched my heart when she said, "Because he was so fearful in the beginning and we had no idea about his history, the only time I would try to gently groom him was while he was eating. And I was very careful to remain in his sight and out of his kick zone. One of the most precious moments between us happened one afternoon while he was eating and I was brushing him. I always sang to him while I brushed him, and on this day I looked at his face and realized he had been finished eating for some time but had kept his precious face in his bucket so I would keep brushing. It was at that moment he had my heart forever! Copper might not know it, but he had just rescued me and made me his."

By the end of September, Copper was very comfortable with her and would even let her kiss his muzzle. For Bethany, the hardest part of taking care of him was leaving him to go home. She hated the thought of him being alone all night, but she had to be thankful for every minute she was with him and every wonderful experience they shared together.

You might think a starved horse would eat anything he was offered, but Copper taught them that even rescues have preferences. He would not eat carrots. What horse doesn't eat carrots? In an effort to find something special to offer him each afternoon, she asked one of her animal-loving cafeteria ladies how much they charged for apples, and, of course, told her who they were for. The lady told Bethany not to worry about buying an apple because the students leave them all over the cafeteria. It was at that moment a new tradition was born. Bethany started what she called the treat trough in their cafeteria where she collected unwanted apples, carrots, and bananas for rescued horses. Special treats became the norm, all because of one picky, adorable stallion. Even now, three years later, she is still collecting bags full of horse treats and delivering them to horse rescues all over the county.

After October had ended and three months of steady groceries were provided, Copper was filling out and looking healthy. Bethany could actually halter him and walk him around the pasture and up hills, trying to build muscle. She was sure Copper enjoyed it as much as she did. She would sing the whole time they walked and even taped a video once. Bethany said, "It's not great, but it's all I have left." After being fed, groomed, and walked, that southern gentleman would walk her back to the gate when she had to leave, and yes, she has a video of that too.

They were able to celebrate Christmas Day together after Bethany's family obligations were finished. She said, "I spent the morning with my family, of course. It was an extremely cold day, so I was happy to get to feed him his hot mash and lots of treats. And in the quiet stillness of the afternoon, I wondered if he knew about baby Jesus and the life-changing significance of that manger in Bethlehem. I never realized the healing power of a barn or an animal until I spent four months with this stallion. I know he was God's gift to my heart right when I needed it the most. I had lost my best friend to pancreatic cancer just three days after Copper arrived. Could he sense my heart was broken? Could he tell that I needed to just sit quietly and love on him while I reflected on the life of one of my closest and dearest friends?"

On January 7, 2014, Copper was found lying on the ground of his shelter, kicking the wall in horrible pain. The vet arrived quickly and found his heart rate very erratic and rapid. Although the symptoms resembled those of colic, the veterinarian was more concerned about his heart, so arrangements were made to have him transported to the University of Georgia's Veterinary Hospital. Knowing how much Bethany loved Copper, they waited for her arrival from school to kiss him goodbye. She didn't know it would be her last goodbye.

Copper's heart rate continued to escalate during the night. He was surrounded by skilled veterinarians and students alike who did their very best to save his life and give him comfort during the pain. And because he stayed alive on monitors through the night, the students were able to gain valuable experience. So even on his last night here on this Earth, he was teaching others. The veterinarians said that because of the neglect he had suffered during his six years of life, his internal organs, especially his heart, had suffered damage. There was nothing else they could do for him, but they were able to learn from him, just as Bethany did. It was not the quantity of the time but the quality of the time they had together. She never owned him. She never rode him. But every minute with him was significant and special. Bethany has always hoped Copper knew how incredibly amazing and loved he was. She said, "He will never be forgotten," and he never has been.

I think horses and other animals come into our lives, brought by the power of the universe at a perfect time to address perfect issues. What Ms. Thomas experienced is a perfect example of the power of the universe to send you what you need when you need it. Copper was there to lessen the pain of loss Bethany experienced with the death of her best friend. Copper was there to fill a hole and teach a lesson.

There will be times when you feel the communication
instead of hearing it.

This next story revisits Jodie Swain of Wilbraham, Massachusetts. She has been blessed in her life to be open to the communication and connections we share with animals.

Jodie and General

GENERAL WAS A HORSE THAT came to Jodie as a foster. She had a friend who'd purchased General through a rescue, and because she had previously been fostering another horse for the same friend, it wasn't a big deal to add one more to the mix. When the transporter opened the side door of the trailer, General and she took one look at each other, and it was love. Jodie could see the relief on his face when she approached. He wasn't nervous, but he had the eye of a horse who knew enough to be suspicious. Jodie kissed his nose and told him, "Welcome home."

Jodie loved every day she had with him. When it came time for the trucker and her to transport General and his partner to his owner, she was sad but hopeful. He was supposed to become a lesson horse. Jodie had advised his owner General might not be what she was looking for. While he was kind, he wasn't particularly patient. He expected you to know what you were doing and respectfully took offense when you didn't. And Jodie sensed that in the wrong hands he would be vengeful. She remained hopeful she might see General again, emitting that energy to all points of the universe.

Jodie said, "General is the kind of horse that would live in your garage. So long as there's some food and water, he'll be happy. I've brought him to horse shows where trainers let me keep him with their horses, and they *all* reported he's just a good citizen. Nothing really makes him nervous. (Well, there are those rocks on the trail that look like they might eat him, but …) I was extra happy when I got to be the one to put him in his new stall. There were fresh shavings and a good load of hay in the corner. I looked around and I was satisfied."

Jodie told me she walked him in, took off his halter, kissed his cheek, and started out the door. To her surprise, General became panicky. He was trying to follow Jodie out of the stall. She stopped, came back in, and hugged his big head, all the time fighting her tears. His owner was occupied with the trucker so she quietly whispered in General's ear, "You be a good boy. But if you want to come back, all you gotta do is scare her. Now, *don't you hurt her* … but if you scare her, she'll give you back."

Jodie told me he winked at her. Seriously, he winked. It took her aback but only for a moment. General looked at her for another moment and then calmly walked over and started working at his hay like it was just another day. Jodie said, "It only took three months, and unfortunately, he did hurt her but not too badly. I did indeed receive that call, and he's been with me ever since." Jodie was absolutely sure General understood every word she said that day, and after talking to her about this, I am in total agreement with her.

Jodie is convinced General hears her plans. She said, "For instance, if I am lunging him, I might think to myself, *When he gets to the barn door I'll have him walk.* I swear to God, each and every time when he gets to the exact spot I was thinking of, he comes down to a walk. I've had to learn to keep one train of thought in the back of my head and a louder thought in front so he can't hear through the noise."

General's communication skill set has come in pretty handy for both him and Jodie. When he is suspicious of something new in his stall, Jodie can just talk to him and tell him to relax and that it's nothing to worry about. And he relaxes every time. Jodie no longer stares at him with mouth agape but instead has come to expect nothing short of complete understanding when she talks to General.

Almost all animal communication is silent, and it cements the connection we share with them. They seem to have the ability to talk to you through thought, and Jodie points this out perfectly. I like to believe General gave her a lesson in silent communication, first by doing what she was thinking, and then, after he had her attention, he showed her how to receive his messages and lessons. He was the perfect teacher.

Don't spend so much time seeking the why
that you fail to enjoy the now.

Starring in this story about animal connections is a horse named Tando, a registered thoroughbred. Tando is owned by Jan Born and at the time of this incident, she and Jan lived in the Santa Clarita Valley of California, just north of Los Angeles.

Tando and the Rattler

TANDO IS A BEAUTIFUL CHESTNUT with a flaxen mane and tail. For those few who are uninitiated to the horse world, flaxen means a pale-yellow mane and tail that stand out in contrast to the darker color of the coat. It might be appropriate that her registered name is Lil Bit of Axe. Given her hard and flinty personality, it fit perfectly. Jan described her as a little distant and not one of those horses that showers you with love and affection. She always did everything asked of her, but in the beginning, Jan had the feeling that Tando didn't particularly like her.

Those feelings may have changed a little in 1985 after Tando did something surprising while being led to a washing rack after a lesson. All of a sudden, Tando stopped walking and would not continue. She stood stock-still and simply wouldn't budge. Jan said, "After trying to pull her forward, coaxing her verbally, and asking what her problem was, I turned to see this fairly large and alert rattlesnake twenty feet ahead, directly in the path of where we were heading. I hadn't seen it before her action pointed it out."

Jan admitted initially thinking Tando probably had her own safety in mind, but upon reflection, her hope lies with Tando having her safety in mind as well. Their relationship continues, and she is still the standoffish mare Jan has come to love for being exactly what she is and nothing more. Nothing entices Tando to act differently, not even carrots or treats, but that is okay. Jan has become extremely comfortable with

Tando being who she is. Jan has never again questioned her safety when she is with Tando. She knows she will be well taken care of.

The day Jan and Tando encountered the rattler, their relationship changed. It became deeper and more accepting of the differences that exist between all beings. We are all different, yet we are still all the same. Our sameness is part of an energy that, to date, cannot be explained by science or considered coincidental by a majority of those who experience it. It is simply synchronicity at its best. Be accepting of the differences existing between all beings. Our differences live only on the surface, so look for the deeper connection. Search for the sameness—the connection that lives inside of each of us. Focus, and you will find it. When you do find it, life changes.

Greet this day knowing
all you need has been placed in front of you.

In this section of the book, we will visit those things that occur way outside the normally understood reality of the world—you know, those things bordering on unbelievable, especially if you tend to give more weight to the scientific side of things. Not being one who believes in coincidence at all, I embrace all possibilities in life, even those that may sound incredible and far-fetched. Meet Diane Firth, who had a strange experience on her farm located about an hour north of Toronto, Ontario.

The Haunted Stall

D IANE SAID, "I WAS BORN a city girl but always dreamed of one day fulfilling my passion of owning a horse and having my own farm. Animals were and still are special, sacred beings to me. I was always bringing home stray cats, hurt birds, and other animals in need. My Irish grandmother told me when I was but six years old that I had the gift within me. Although I never knew what that meant, I knew that it sounded good."

Finally, in 1995 Diane's dream came true, and the Firth family bought a thirty-acre farm and century-old house. The farm was located off the beaten path in a very remote area. It was surrounded by trees, and if you didn't know where to look, you would not see the farmhouse. A long tree-lined drive led up to the two-story early 1900s block house complete with widow's walk and storm cellar. Built around 1868, the barn was a large bank barn that was hurting for some loving care and had a star protection symbol carved into its side. To the north, the farm lane ran down to their own river. To the west was miles of land running toward the Niagara Escarpment. It was a quiet piece of heaven with a lot of privacy and acres for their two horses to run.

The farm had been listed for sale for many months with no bidders. It would need many hours of sweat equity to repair it to its glory days, but the price was right. They discovered that the last farm owner died in the 1950s, and since then, the farm had been rented out to a series of tenants; some lasted a year, some just a few months. The farm had been sitting vacant for the past year. But there was something about the feel, the look of the house, and the land that said to them, "Please love me." And just like that, they became farm owners. Diane rented a horse van, and one sunny day in late fall, they all moved in.

Diane had this to say about the horses' arrival: "It would be easy to say all was perfect, but I remember unlocking the door to the house that first day, surveying the disrepair and the peeling layers of wallpaper, and thinking, *Oh my God, I can't live here. What have we done?* The horses must have picked up my vibes because it was a fight just to get them out of the trailer to enter the barn door. They neighed and nickered and snorted, refusing to go in. With some gentle coaxing with carrots and oats, they hesitantly made their way inside; their hooves echoed as they walked down the aisle. Shane snorted and backed up as he walked by the first stall, and Trim made a point to give the stall an extra wide berth."

Life evolved for the Firth family. A friend of theirs from the race track rented out several stalls for layovers from the track, injuries, and mares due to foal. They installed better lighting and tried to take away the dark shadows around the entrance and that first stall.

As time went on, Diane began to notice small incidents occurring. Lights would flicker on and off. Brushes and combs would be misplaced. Water buckets would come off their hooks during the night. The horses had already picked up on the vibes. They demonstrated it whenever she put them in the crossties by the first stall to brush and curry them. They would move around restlessly, stomping their hoofs, snorting, and kicking out. After several mishaps, the blacksmith and the vet finally started using the crossties at the other end of the barn, claiming that it was brighter, and honestly, the horses were calmer there than they were beside the first stall.

Diane was alone one night and had gone out to the barn to tend to one of the horses from the track. She needed to unwrap, massage, apply liniment, and rewrap his front and hind legs. All was going well when all of a sudden Diane began to feel uncomfortable, and the horse also moved about skittishly. Diane felt a draft from above her, and then it was like a heavy, dark, choking weight fell upon her. The horse reared, backed up, broke the bottle of liniment, and leg wraps went flying. He broke the crossties and stood visibly shaking several feet away from her. Fearful that the horse would get hurt, her first reaction was for him, but she couldn't shake the black, dark, boding vibration from above. Looking up, Diane noticed a huge mouth of blackness above her where the ceiling had been. Well, the hairs on her neck and arms were really standing up by then. Was someone there? Was someone going to attack her? Diane slowly realized the black mouth was the door to the hay chute that now lay open, and she was looking up two stories into the darkness. Well, there was no way she planned to go up into the mound in the dark to investigate. Instead, she left a note for hubby to always remember to lock the hay chute after using it. The next evening, everything was back in order.

On a mild evening in late September, Diane had opened the windows in their bedroom to allow for a fresh flow of air. At about two o'clock in the morning their dog Ki jumped up on the bed barking and growling. At first dazed, Diane soon picked up a commotion coming from the barn—boards breaking, horses crying out, things making banging noises, and more. Terrified that someone was trying to steal the horses, they quickly dressed, grabbed flashlights, and ran up to the barn. The barn door was still closed and latched, so whatever or whoever was there had come in another way.

Turning on the lights, they found one of the geldings in the first stall had kicked half his door off the hinges, one hoof had tangled in his water bucket, and several of the side boards had been cracked in two. He was frantic, bleeding where the boards had cut his legs, and trapped by the bucket. Several hours later, he had settled down in another stall, and they had the vet coming to check his leg. They decided to stop using the stall, at the time mainly due to the cost of repairs.

In mid-November, it happened again. The commotion woke them immediately and they literally flew up to the barn. Again, the barn door was closed and latched. They tried the light switch, but nothing came on. They could feel crushed glass on the floor. Terrified, Diane shined the flashlight on the first stall. The horse in that stall was down, thrashing on the floor, and her back hoofs were sticking through the side boards, where she had kicked through the wall, trapping her legs. Diane's husband motioned her to look up to the hay chute; the trapdoor was open, and just the ends of a rope dangled down from above.

Diane said, "To describe the fear and panic, it strangled me. I was worried not only for the horse but also for whatever else was happening in this barn. It was becoming overwhelming." They got the horse freed and back on her legs, and their vet paid yet another visit to treat her cuts and abrasions. Diane's partner and she thoroughly checked out the loft the next morning. The sliding doors of the bank were still closed and fastened. There was some disarray with the hay bales but no more than a family of raccoons could cause. The door to the hay chute was closed and fastened, and when they looked inside, the trapdoor was back in place and fastened and the rope hung as usual on its hook.

To say the barn and the horses now had their attention would be an understatement. They began talking back over the incidents and unanimously agreed to forgo using that stall. They installed a two-way monitor between the barn and the house to pick up any nightly noises and grew more concerned after just a few nights of listening. The horses were restless and uncomfortable, nickering, kicking, snorting, and were glad to get out of the barn each morning. They even started leaving a light on in the barn every night.

Diane asked their vet if he had heard any strange stories about the property, and he suggested she talk to some of the older local farmers. She checked out the local newspaper office, but their files only went back to the 1960s. One older local did remember some strange talk from his younger years about a possible death or murder but admitted it was all kind of cloudy.

Diane started booby-trapping the door to the hay chute, strategically placing pieces of hay or straw to see if anyone opened the door. Some mornings she would find the hay moved and other days not. Then she began questioning herself and wondering if it had simply been a breeze or a mouse. Diane is a gem hound, so she decided to place some pieces of rose quartz and smoky quartz by the hay chute door (at least they were heavier, and a breeze wouldn't blow them away). No changes for almost two weeks, and then she discovered that the stones and been moved or shoved away from the door, and one rose quartz was missing.

It became their belief that something bad had happened in the barn, and their feelings were validated by their intuition and the actions of the horses that stayed in it. They never housed another horse in that first stall. They turned off the hydro connection for the lights by the hay chute and over time switched to using the back barn door for the horses.

Shane and Trim crossed the rainbow bridge a few years later, and their friend bought his own farm. Once again, the barn sat neglected and empty, the barn boards beginning to wear in the winds, and the metal roofing taking a beating in storms. Was there a spirit still in the barn, trapped between the veils of reality and the unknown? Had someone met an untimely death in the barn? Was there a murder to remain unsolved forever? There were many questions without answers. Like Diane, I like to listen to my voice inside for answers to those questions, and intuition generally has an answer.

Diane said, "We eventually moved away from the area. The rose quartz stone was never found. As for the barn, she still stands empty— or what is left of her."

Diane's glimpse behind the veil is open to interpretation, but do so with a mind open to the possibility that more exists in this world than you have ever been taught. I know when I first started having strange, post-diagnosis experiences, I didn't tell anyone. As my friend from England, Anne Duff, would say, some might think I'd lost the plot. (I love the English twist of words.) I didn't discuss it because I wasn't sure I believed what I actually saw. It took time to accept that things were not as I'd been taught. This I know, and Diane learned: once you are open to possibilities, the more you will witness. Diane's husband passed away in June 2018. She has a night-light in her bedroom, and every night, the light flicks off and on. Her intuition tells her that her husband is saying goodnight. I know I believe. You?

I am not what I was when this journey began.
I am what I became after life's lessons were learned.

In this time of computers, internet, and social media, we are blessed to meet people from all over the world, and I have met many primarily due to my love of animals, especially horses. Some of these people, whom I have never met in person, have become longtime friends.

Kevan Garecki of British Columbia, Canada, is one of these people—a cowboy who understands not only the horse but also the kingdom of animals with whom we coexist in this universe. Early in 2017, while researching the idea for this book, I contacted Kevan to see if he had any experiences in his life with animals that defied science and coincidence, and lucky for us, he did. It is a masterful, true accounting about a little girl and some magic reindeer.

Reindeer Magic

EVEN THOUGH KEVAN HAD BEEN witness to many amazing things in the company of animals, he had little idea as he traveled along Highway 97, surrounded by pure white snow and bright sunshine, that it would become one of the most magical days of his existence on this sphere we call home.

He drove slowly, ever mindful of the passengers in his trailer. Although a little out of the ordinary for him being a horse hauler, he was transporting a pair of reindeer back home to Dawson Creek for the owners. They had been in the Frazer Valley area of southern British Columbia for two months during a promotional event. He was traveling complete with a sign on the back of the trailer that had been given to him by a friend. It said: "Shhh ... Reindeer Sleeping!" The sign garnered a lot of attention during the trip, but no one had any idea how important the words on the sign would be to one special little person.

Pulling into the parking lot of a Tim Horton's in Williams Lake, British Columbia, Kevan found himself hungry and sorely in need of a good stretching of the legs, not to mention needing a bit more caffeine.

Being a consummate professional and knowing his first responsibility was to the animals in his charge, he exited the truck and walked to the trailer to check on the reindeer. He noticed a sedan parked behind his rig and saw a man and small girl reading the sign on the rear of the trailer. After a little encouragement from her father, the little girl started asking questions. The first one was to ask if Kevan could open the back of the trailer so she could see the reindeer. The reply, although not what the little girl wanted to hear, still made her eyes go wide with excitement.

Kevan told her, "Oh no, I couldn't do that. If we opened that hatch, why those reindeer would just fly right on out of there!" Although initially crestfallen, she took possession of the flying reindeer possibility and owned it; magic lit up her eyes and painted a huge smile across her face.

Having seen the look of disappointment that first sprouted on the little girl's face, Kevan offered a substitute. He promised to open the small side door so she could see the reindeer but they couldn't fly out. From the look of excitement on the little girl's face, Kevan knew without doubt that this was a good alternative in her eyes, and she quickly led the way to the side door. She was ready to see some magical flying reindeer.

Kevan expected the reindeer to be close to the door, waiting for a treat, and they didn't disappoint him. As the little girl moved toward the open door, one of the reindeer was ready to peek out. To the amazement and wonder of the girl, their noses touched briefly before both retreated back to look at one another.

The little girl exclaimed, "Dad, I'm touching a reindeer!" while stroking the soft face of the animal.

The father said, "Thank you for this. You've really made her day. She'll have quite a story to tell—" He was cut off before finishing by the woman (apparently his wife) who curtly told him that they were running close on time and had to go and go now. From the tone of her voice and mannerisms, he knew his time visiting with the girl was over … for now.

As the girl left with her father, Kevan went about his job of caring for the animals. He got them some fresh water and replenished their alfalfa before taking care of himself. As he was attending to the reindeer, he was privy to a conversation between the man and his wife. From what they were saying, the little girl needed to go to a hospital and had to be there before three o'clock. Kevan started putting things together. The little girl had a head cover on, and he suddenly realized that he hadn't seen any hair protruding from under it. That and her pale complexion led him to believe that she might be living with cancer or some other debilitating illness, and sadness washed over him.

So much pain in this world; children should never face things like this, or so he thought. He also, begrudgingly, realized that we do not know near what we think we know about life and living, and maybe, just maybe, things are happening just the way they are supposed to, painful or not. With a glance at the sky and an utterance about the worsening weather, Kevan pulled out and continued on so he could get the reindeer home before getting stuck in another snowstorm.

Kevan made good time regardless of the intermittent snow showers until he made Bijou Falls at the southern base of Pine Pass. Easing on the throttle, Kevan coaxed the rig up the mountain just as the snow started in earnest. In order to have the reindeer home by the promised time, he had to keep moving. Slow but safe was his goal.

Up ahead, he could barely make out the dim headlights of a car on the side of the road, and he slowed down to offer assistance. Parking his rig and making his way through the snow, Kevan was surprised to see the same family and the same wide-eyed little girl. He found himself a little overcome with emotions when he saw her and quickly came to the realization that the reindeer were going to be a little late.

Kevan listened as the man explained that the car simply stopped right where it was and wouldn't start again. He got the car as far off the road as possible and into a snowbank, and there it would be until they could make arrangements with a towing service. The problem was that there wasn't a towing service or a town nearby, and they needed to get to the hospital. Moreover, the little girl looked cold and weak. Kevan let the family know that the weather was getting worse, and the best thing to do was to get in his truck, and he would take them to the hospital where they could call a tow truck. They braved the swirling snow and wind and made their way back to the truck. After a quick check on the reindeer, Kevan got underway once again with the new charges and their gear.

Twenty minutes later, things took a turn for the worse. The knowledge of this downturn came with a scream from the back seat. "Kaitlyn! I can't wake her up!"

Even though the truck's heater was trying mightily, the thirty-below-zero temperatures were taxing it beyond its ability to heat the interior of the truck. In the back seat, the parents had to get to work to keep their daughter from going into hypothermia. This meant trying skin-to-skin contact with the little girl between her parents.

A glimpse by the driver to the back seat painted a vivid picture of worried parents. Kevan noticed the father's salt-and-pepper hair and the worried lines on his face and realized the toll the girl's illness had taken on her parents. The father was stoic in his mannerisms, whereas the wife was understandably angry and didn't mind who knew it. Kevan continued making progress, albeit very slow progress, and kept a watchful eye on his backseat passengers.

It was about thirty minutes after the parents had started warming their daughter that the truck was suddenly rocked by a strong gust of wind, and a complete and total whiteout began. Progress slowed to a virtual creep, and vison was down to a mere few feet. Kevan spotted a side road and guided the truck and trailer off the road until conditions improved. He explained to the parents that for the moment, this was as far as they could travel safely.

"I'm gonna give you folks some privacy and go check on the reindeer." He grabbed an old heavy parka and exited the relative warmth of his truck. As soon as he left the truck, he was hit with a brutally cold wind that sucked the very air from his lungs. Simply breathing was a chore. Huddled in the trailer as far from any wind as they could possibly get, Kevan realized that the cold was even harder on the reindeer than he had thought possible. They had spent a month in the southern part of British Columbia, and the warmer temperatures had fooled their coats into thinking it was spring; they had started to shed their winter coats and had each dropped one antler. The cold was biting them no matter where they tried to hide. The driver went about spreading bedding on the floor as insulation and closing all the vents save one in the rear. Kevan had a little talk with the reindeer before exiting the trailer and making his way back to the relative comfort and safety of the truck cab.

Upon reentering the truck to see the little girl awake and aware, Kevan was momentarily relieved. The girl smiled at him weakly, and seeing her smile made him realize that she desperately needed to be in a hospital and not on the side of the road in a blizzard. The little girl reached forward and took Kevan's hand in hers. It was then that he realized without doubt that this precious little girl would die if he didn't get her to a hospital fairly quickly. He started talking to the girl in an attempt to keep her awake and give her something to think about besides her illness.

"So, betcha no one in your neighborhood is gonna believe it when you tell 'em you petted a real, live reindeer!"

The little girl smiled again and then spoke so softly the driver couldn't make out a word. As he leaned closer, she repeated, "Are those real reindeer?"

"Well, they look mighty real to me!" Kevan replied and then added "Oh, you mean are they like Santa's reindeer—all magic an' everything?"

The girl nodded slowly in response.

"Well, of course they are! Hey, all reindeer are magic, you know, but only the ones with the strongest magic get to go to work for Santa!" At this, the girl's eyes widened slightly, so the man continued, "See, Santa has a lot of work to do in a real short time, so he needs all the extra magic around him he can get. That's why he picks reindeer like these two to help out!"

"Where does their magic come from?" the girl asked quietly.

The man leaned back closer to the girl as he answered, "Ya gotta promise never to tell a soul what I'm about to say. Understand?"

The girl's eyes widened again as she listened intently.

"It all comes from their antlers. And every year 'bout this time they've used up most of the magic in 'em, so that's why reindeers shed their antlers cuz the magic's almost used up! Oh, there's still plenty left over in some of them, though. In fact, I've got one right here if you want to scc it."

The girl struggled to sit up but could only manage a reclining position leaning against her father's chest. The driver had collected two of the antlers shed by the reindeer earlier; he reached behind his seat to retrieve one of them and laid it across the child's lap. She gazed in wonderment as she stroked the convoluted surface of each tine. As she investigated the antler, Kevan continued his story.

"See, the ones with the real good magic, their antlers always keep some behind after they've fallen off, so you're holdin' onto some real, live reindeer magic right there!" He watched the look of amazement on the little girl's face as she held and studied the antler. The girl rolled the antler around once more and then reluctantly offered it back to the driver. He reached for it but suddenly retreated, saying, "You best hang onto that for the time being. I need you to look after all that magic for us cuz we're sure gonna need it tonight!" He offered a look of mock concern.

The girl looked to her father, who simply nodded as he brushed his hand across her now rapidly flushing cheeks. The girl sighed as she brought the antler close to her body and then slowly closed her eyes.

Finally, the snow abated enough for the driver to see the sides of the roadway, and he knew he could keep the truck between the ditches. Time to put much-needed initiative in motion but this time for a greater need; with that, the trek to the hospital began in earnest. One bit of good news was that there was no traffic to contend with or any abandoned vehicles to bar their progress.

As it normally does, persistence paid off with success, and they pulled into the entrance to the emergency room. Kevan had called ahead, and there were two nurses waiting for them in the warm and inviting interior of this house of hope and healing. The nurses rushed the little girl into the relative comfort of the hospital, followed very closely by her parents, leaving Kevan behind, watching their backs rapidly recede.

Making his way to a parking area, his head was full of thoughts and questions about what to do now. After parking, he went back to the trailer to check on the reindeer. As he was working on their comfort, his mind was racing. Some of his thoughts unfortunately brought old hurts to the forefront of his mind. Those hurts are never deep below the surface, and some pain never completely goes away but waits to serve as a reminder of loss. He continued working on the reindeers' comfort in the cold trailer and talked to them as he worked.

"You girls rest now," he muttered and then had an afterthought. He bent down to the eldest reindeer and begged a favor. "Lady, I don't know what reindeer do when they're needing help, but I'd sure appreciate anything you can do for that little girl." He paused as his eyes began to mist, despite his efforts to hold back the tears. Not knowing entirely why, he felt he needed to explain his own sense of urgency to the small creatures looking curiously at him. He paused for a moment then said, "I can't bear those folks to go through what I did, ya know? Just ain't right. Parents shouldn't have to outlive their own babies!"

His mind drifted for a time, thinking back to his own daughter, gone now for so many years, yet the pain of her loss was still sharp. The man bowed his head briefly and was surprised to find both reindeer looking intently into his eyes as he raised his head. He was unsure what to make of that, but he stepped from the trailer thinking he had just experienced something quite unusual indeed ... Who knows what magic the universe had in store for that cold and blustery winter's night?

Just for a moment, Kevan left the cold of the trailer and sat back down in the warm cab of the truck to think. There, he was surprised to see the antler he had given the little girl lying on the back seat, and he knew what he had to do. He grabbed the antler and braved the cold wind and snow as he headed back into the hospital. A snowy gale pursued him through the doors as he walked into the building. The admitting nurse looked up grimly and then recognized the man. She nodded as she stood up to greet him and give him directions to the little girl's room. Kevan explained that he was not family and should probably just sit in the waiting room for a bit. Remembering what he held in his hand, he turned back to the nurse and asked her if she could please make sure the little girl received the antler in his hand.

The nurse looked quizzically from it to the man, and then her gaze softened as she nodded in understanding. These types of pleas were viewed as last requests and never taken lightly. The nurse reached for the antler, pursed her lips while nodding once again to the man, and then turned toward the entrance of the examining room.

As promised, the nurse took the antler into the little girl's room, and Kevan found the most comfortable chair he could see and sat down to await news, good or bad, with energy toward the good. The nurse questioned the attending doctor with her eyes only, and he indicated she could give the antler to the resting little girl. When placed on her bed, the little girl awoke and spotted the antler, and her eyes widened before slowly closing once again. Everyone was watching the little girl's reaction, and had they not been, they might not have missed seeing a slight spike in her vital signs … After a few minutes, the doctor rose, looked at the parents, and told them he would leave them in privacy with their daughter. He told them that he had done all he could do for her, and he bowed his head and left the room.

As the doctor stepped into the admitting room, Kevan stood up and looked expectantly toward him. He stood there for a moment waiting for the doctor to look his way, but when he did, he just looked at the floor and shook his head before turning away to walk out of the room. The driver stood there with clenched fists, hating to feel so helpless. A mixture of rage and anguish boiled through him as he paced the waiting room. Thoughts of the tale he told the girl about the reindeer magic trickled in, making the man begin to wish fervently that such things were actually true. The evening wore on in this fashion, with the man's reflections often turning to what he simply regarded as hopeful folly.

At one point, Kevan dozed off; his dreams were bizarre, as is often the trademark of an uneasy nap. His slumber was suddenly interrupted when he heard a cry from the next room. The doctor was the first to wheel around as he sprinted from his desk toward the examining room with his nurses close behind. As they parted the curtain shrouding the girl's bed, they were met with a most unexpected sight indeed. A pair of unusually bright eyes greeted them as the girl seemed to almost glow. Almost at once, the staff recognized the momentary rally that was often the final stage before a forgiving death that many of us have witnessed or heard about. They fought to maintain a professional air as the parents dared to smile, thinking their daughter was going to live.

The doctor was performing a cursory check of the array of instruments collected in the room when he noticed what he thought must have been a minor anomaly in the readings. As he rechecked the various displays, he began to see a subtle but distinct pattern; the girl's vital signs were indeed improving, although he was at a complete loss to explain why. He beckoned one of the nurses over to look at what he was seeing, as much for reassurance as anything else. After looking over the previous readings, they both compared those with what the machines indicated.

The nurse slowly lifted her head to stare into the perplexed eyes of the doctor. Being of native descent, perhaps she was more in touch with her spiritual side, or maybe she just felt something that was out of place in that sterile and logical world. The nurse nodded to the antler as she quietly said, "Maybe we got some help we weren't counting on."

The doctor looked in the direction of her gaze and shrugged his shoulders. "Well if so, I sure won't chase it away!" he stated, trying to inject as much cheer as he could muster.

As they turned to regard their patient, the girl smiled briefly as she looked at them and then offered the antler, asking, "Have you ever seen a reindeer antler?"

The nurse smiled as she bent down to take a closer look, "Why no!" she admitted. "I had no idea what that was," she went on truthfully.

As the nurse stroked the surface of the antler, something stirred deep inside her; ancient voices murmured long-forgotten chants, and ethereal glimpses of otherworldly beings flitted past as distant memories began to cascade through her mind. Her father was known among the people for his many unique abilities. He was what the new faces to the land called a shaman. His voice cooed softly in her mind: "Remember, child: that which cannot be seen or felt is every bit as real as the ground under your feet. The spirits are always here. They can either help or hinder, and the choice is ours."

As the vision faded, the nurse was left with a strong feeling of being joined in the room by a multitude. So powerful was the sensation that she was prompted to look around her. Preoccupied, the nurse had been completely unaware of the man standing in the doorway. Arising and going to the doorway to the girl's room, Kevan was seemingly on a mission known only to him. He paused at the doorway and watched as the woman in the hospital scrubs seemed to be daydreaming, but even the small measure of Déné blood in him knew better. He felt the waft from behind the veil and knew what it meant. As the sensation swept over him, the driver listened to echoes from his upbringing and joined in the experience, lending his own spirit to the multitude.

As he did so, the sensation grew to envelop even the parents who now held the child's hands. They looked from each other to the driver and nurse, realizing there was something happening that was beyond their understanding, yet neither was fearful. Instead, they watched with curious intent as the two before them stood in apparent ignorance of all else surrounding them. The enclosure took on a hushed tone, as the forest might after a heavy snowfall. The only sounds were the soft plinks of the machines as they droned their digital incantations. The sole movement in the room was the undulation of the scanners while they displayed the child's vital signs.

Both the nurse and the man continued their reverie until an unspoken signal lifted the veil. The nurse looked around to discover she was the focus of the parents' gaze. She shuffled and then brushed her hands against her scrubs in an effort to appear more professional. This caused the driver to emerge from his own trance, and both exchanged a meaningful look. He simply nodded and then averted his stare to the young girl who lay in the bed between them. As he did, the girl stirred and returned his look. She smiled at the driver and slowly lifted the antler for him to see that she was still caring for it. He nodded in approval to her and then winked just before slipping from the room.

Making his way to the admitting desk, Kevan inquired as to the whereabouts of the washroom. As the attendant directed him, the nurse from the examining room caught his eye. She jerked her head slightly, beckoning him to follow her. As he did, she turned and regarded him carefully before asking if he felt what happened in the hospital room, He nodded once, which was all the recognition needed between them.

The nurse lowered her head, pondering the experience, and after a thoughtful moment, she looked him in the eyes again and said, "I guess we both know what went on in there."

The driver nodded once again and put his hand on her shoulder as he began to explain, "These things happen for a reason, and we don't have to spoil it by intellectualizing anything. Besides, I don't know that there's much to explain anyway. We both know what happened, right?" he returned with a wink.

They both stood silently, each in turn taking in what the event meant to them when the sound of laughter gently pushed the moment aside. They exchanged glances before turning their attention to the examining room once more. A man's chuckle prompted them to investigate, and upon entering the enclosure, they were met by a most welcome scene indeed. There sat the family, drawn closely together, holding hands and joking. The girl looked not only far stronger than only moments before but seemed too healthy to be in that hospital. The nurse strode forward to check the monitors and looked up in amazement. Where only hours before lay a child on the edge of death, now a body filled with vigor sat smiling back at her, and the readings only served to prove what could not be otherwise verified. She looked to the driver, who simply smiled and then nodded to the antler.

Feeling she was being watched, the girl turned to the driver and then extended both arms, inviting him toward her. The man glanced to the father first and then hesitantly made his way to the bedside. As he drew within reach of those tiny arms, the girl wiggled her fingers to draw the man closer. Emotions flooded through him as his mind flashed back to his own daughter who once beckoned him in much the same way. He bent down to receive a surprisingly robust hug from the little girl, and strangely enough, he did not feel the need to pull back. No need to escape the innocent honesty that comes from a child.

"Thank you," whispered the tiny girl as she relaxed her hug on the man.

Kevan explained that is wasn't anything he did but was instead the magic of the reindeer. The girl smiled at him and offered a tiny wink of her own before looking down almost sadly at the antler. At length, she raised it toward the driver's hand and looked over, waiting for him to take it. He stood still for only a moment before gently pushing the antler back to the girl.

"I do believe that belongs to you now," he smiled.

The girl looked up in disbelief as the man explained that he had had a talk with the reindeer and she wanted the little girl to keep the antler safe until she worked up enough magic to grow a new one next year.

The girl looked up as a sly grin emerged across her face, "Are you sure?" she chided, followed by doubts about reindeer talking to him.

The driver mustered up a look of feigned admonishment and said, "Well of course they can! Ya just gotta know what to listen for!"

The child fell silent for a moment and then asked him if that is what he and the nurse were doing earlier—listening. He felt a flush in his cheeks as he turned to see the nurse staring at him. They shared only a brief glance before Kevan returned his attention to the girl, telling her that they were just waiting for the magic to work because it works every time. He was rewarded by a very bright little girl smile.

The next morning dawned as only a northern winter day can—crystal clear and hushed from the deep mantle of fresh snow that lay over the town. Kevan emerged from the hospital and paused as the sunlight spilled across his weathered face. He was enjoying the feeling of the meager warmth when his attention suddenly reverted to his passengers, along with a good dose of worry for not checking on them sooner.

He trudged his way around the building to find the rig humming its single staccato note to itself, and leaned up to peer into the window of the trailer. The younger reindeer looked up expectantly at the man and blinked. As he eased inside, the elder of the two raised herself slowly and shook off the night's rest, and then she stared intently at Kevan as if questioning him.

"Ya done good, Mom," came the meaningful reply to her gaze. He stroked her neck softly as she continued to stare up at him, then she nudged his arm gently as she made her way over to the other reindeer, who coincidently was her own daughter. In a simple display, the two gently touched noses before turning to face him in unison.

He felt the small animals were acting out some expression, when suddenly a vision of his daughter blended into his consciousness so vividly that for an instant he thought she was actually standing before him. As the apparition faded, the elder reindeer walked slowly toward him, looked down briefly, and then shook her head to shed her remaining antler. He stood very still for a moment, and then in a quivering voice, he asked, "Is that … for me?" The reindeer simply bowed her head and backed away, leaving the antler laying at his feet.

Addendum

There was a time ten or so years ago when I would have believed this to be a pretty darn good work of fiction. Then things happened in my life that enabled me to see the gray areas of life that lie between black and white, right and wrong, the known and unknown. The world became a much larger and a much more magical place to live—a place of many possibilities and amazing wonder.

When the idea for this book was born, I reached out to my horse friends and animal lovers for stories that defied science, defied coincidence (the latter of which I do not believe in), and that smacked you up beside your head with a sparkly unicorn wand in order to get your attention. I know because I have experienced them, that many others, if paying attention, have experienced them as well.

Kevan was one of the first people I contacted to see if he had any experiences with animals that mirrored some of mine. This story is exactly what I was looking for, and Kevan was gracious enough to let me use his experience. The only changes I made were to the point of view. Kevan originally told the story from a first-person point of view because he was present for the occurrences. I tell a story from the third person point of view, that of someone telling a story they have been told.

This I can assure you: this story is true from start to finish, and there were many people who were witnesses to the incident. I am at a place in my life where this is reality to me, and I believe without doubt. How about you?

Magical possibilities live where hope
is fueled by faith. With this combination,
all things are possible.

Let us take a trip to the West Coast, specifically to Costa Mesa, California, and visit with Tammy Iglehart. We will hear about her otherworldly experience with her Jack Russell terrier, Turbo. We will see the amazing synchronicities she encountered after his death.

Tammy is a licensed physical therapist and athletic trainer. Her philosophy is in line with natural healing and communication. Her specialties are osteopathic manual therapy, craniosacral therapy, and sports medicine. Tammy is one of those highly educated people who believes in magic. I met her through her sister Becky, who is a cowgirl and a very talented photographer.

Remembering Turbo

To set the stage, Tammy lost her beloved Jack Russell terrier, Turbo, to a tragic accident. He was nine years old when he escaped one day and was involved in one of his favorite pastimes: chasing rabbits. He was so into the chase he failed to recognize they were about to cross a road. He was hit by a car, and just like that, life in Tammy's house changed dramatically. The journey that began when Turbo was eight weeks old and lasted until he was nine years old came to a sad and abrupt end. The memories he left behind became as valuable as gold.

Tammy had this to say about Turbo: "It was a devastating blow, and it left a giant hole in my world. We had been through five moves together and many life changes, both good and bad. He was my constant companion and partner. We spoke a silent language of understanding. Our hearts were connected."

After Turbo's death, Tammy missed him so much that she knew she wanted another dog in her life. She wanted another from the same breeder she got Turbo from. The original breeder had retired and sold his breeding stock to Brent Hopkins of Colorado. Tammy called him and discovered he'd just had a litter born that would be ready in six weeks. A major plus was these puppies were from the same stud dog as Turbo.

Tammy wanted a male. The litter was composed of five females and one male. Tammy put her deposit down on the male, and Brent sent her pictures of her chosen one. The pup was the twin image of Turbo. Both of them had the same sized patch of brown over their left eyes and a small curl of color on the leading edge of their right ears. To look at their faces, you would think it was the same dog with pictures taken at different times of growth. It was like a reincarnation of Turbo. Tammy said, "I was in shock when I saw the photo. He was the spitting image of Turbo as a pup. I was filled with emotion; the tears fell as I felt a combination of sorrow and great joy at the same time."

Tammy had this to say about the events leading to her deciding to get two puppies that day: "As the weeks went on before the pickup, I talked to many Jack Russell terrier owners and was convinced that raising two pups was actually easier, as they would entertain each other, keep each other company, and not become so attached and anxious when left alone. It was true. So, I called Brent and told him that I wanted to get a female as well. I would pick her out when I met them at the Ernie pick up."

After Tammy arrived, Brent brought her the male, and it was love at first sight. Tammy said that the empty place she had held in her heart began to fill on first contact. She said, "He licked my face and looked in my eyes, and it was an instant bond and already unbreakable. Picking out the female was a bit more challenging, but Tammy simply went with the one that came to her to play. The male became Ernie and the female Ruby. And so, life began anew for the pups and Tammy as they made their way back to California.

About four months after this menagerie set up housekeeping in California, something happened that caused some deep and personal reflection in Tammy. It was so powerful Tammy can still remember the date. It was September 29, the anniversary of Turbo's birth. On this particular morning, it was business as usual; get up, pups go outside for potty time, puppy breakfast, and the rest of the morning routine. As the puppies played in the front room, sometimes loudly, Tammy started and patiently waited for her morning coffee.

She noticed that things had gotten quiet. From past experience, Tammy knew quiet usually equaled mischief. As she turned from the counter to go and see what they were into, she was met with the eyes of Ernie. He was standing in the doorway, and he had the most solemn look in his eyes that bordered upon sad. In his mouth rested Turbo's collar. The collar had been residing on Turbo's cremated remains, and Ernie had carefully removed the collar from the container, as it still sat exactly as she had left it.

Tammy said, "He dropped the collar on the floor, and as I picked it up, these sweet puppy eyes communicated with the understanding and kindness of an old, wise soul. I began to weep. They were Turbo's eyes. The life I had with him was there in those big brown eyes. A piece of him was still with me. Ruby and Ernie had been born within a four-day window of Turbo's death. I believe Turbo continued to live through Ernie's soul, as so many similarities presented throughout his life. They liked the same spot on the couch, played the same way with toys, even snuggled in bed in the same spot." Turbo came home through Ernie, and a wondrous reunion it was.

Life went on in the Iglehart home for another seven years, and then Ernie was diagnosed with lung cancer. He was failing fast and sure, and the decision, after much back-and-forth self-questioning, was made to let him cross the bridge and halt the suffering. As sad as the time was, Tammy thought Ruby would need the company of another dog. Cash, a cattle dog of mixed breed, became the newest member of the family.

Over the next six months, Ruby's health started a steep and relatively rapid decline that was sad to watch. Although at first, they could not come up with a solid diagnosis, they finally seemed to lock in on canine dementia. Ruby would start crying for no known reason, and she was getting aggressive with Cash, who at the time was still a small puppy. Tammy said, "I think she was just heartbroken after losing Ernie. The two of them had spent their lives together, so it seemed as if half of her was suddenly gone. It was a very difficult decision to put her down."

Tammy, being an ultimate animal lover, now has Cash, a border terrier named Carter, and an old shepherd mix rescue dog named Alex. Oh, she also lives with all the memories gifted her by the many animals in her life. She said, "Dogs are the best company and create many beautiful life lessons and stories."

I, for one, am very happy Tammy was open to seeing things others may look at briefly but fail to see their real message. Sometimes, we have to unlearn in order to learn, and sometimes we have to quit fearing the reality that the universe keeps showing us.

> I discovered magic. It was living in the same house
> with belief, right next door to possibilities.

Meet Jane Piilola and Jerry Densel who live outside Lincoln, Montana, also the home of Ted (the Unabomber) Kaczynski and Doug Swingley, a four-time Iditarod winner. At one time, they had more than 150 sled dogs in the Lincoln Valley and were highly involved in the sledding dog world. They are also surrounded by a menagerie of other animals. They live in an area that can only be described as an outdoor paradise, frequented daily by deer and randomly by large herds of elk. They are grateful that visits by grizzly bears and mountain lions happen, but they are infrequent. Along with the wildlife, they nurture several chickens, a horse, a dog, a few turkeys, a bunch of feral bunnies, and a large variety of migrating birds, including hummingbirds.

Duck, Duck, Goose

IN MARCH 2013 THREE CHILDREN who had been visiting their grandparents who lived close by showed up with three tiny fluffy ducks. They had discovered the ducks while out gopher hunting, and they told their grandparents the adults had never returned to the nest. Their grandparents told them they had no place to keep them, but Jerry Densel, the man who lived down the road a half mile, loved all kinds of birds and might have room for them. Well, Jerry and Jane could not resist downy, fluffy baby ducks, so they agreed to keep them. They thought they were adopting the birds, but they were wrong on two counts. The first was that they were not baby ducks but were actually baby geese. And the second was that they did not adopt the geese; the geese adopted them.

As they grew, the geese followed them everywhere; nothing was safe from their curiosity. They were terrified of the water, but with the help of Jane and Jerry's two dogs, they soon learned to swim in the pond and became like regular Canadian geese. However, they were unaware they were geese because they had been raised with dogs, humans, and chickens. Not knowing their true parentage, they became the children of every animal and human in their environment. Likewise, they were accepted by every other animal. They followed the dogs everywhere, and when Jane and Jerry appeared in the yard, they followed them around as well. The geese even talked to them in a soft, murmuring talk that Jane and Jerry had never heard before.

In 2014 at the age of fourteen, their older dog, Windy, began having severe seizures. She had one in the house and then went outside and proceeded to seize violently in the driveway. Jerry was outside with the other dog, and Jane was inside. There was nothing they could do but watch tearfully. Magically, the three geese had other ideas. They surrounded the seizing dog and began to murmur to her in their soft voices and kept murmuring to her until the seizure ended. Amazingly, this seizure did not last as long as the others had. Their soft voices provided a source of comfort to her. They lost Windy very shortly after this episode, but they were comforted by the fact that the geese had known what to do for her in her final struggles.

As the geese matured, they would disappear for a time and then reappear. One time only two returned, and then only one returned. They call the remaining goose Grace because she is so amazing. She will be gone for several days and then return with a mate and then disappear and then reappear. She continues to follow them all over, although her mate doesn't know quite what to make of it. When they feed her in the morning, they swear she uses that soft murmuring voice to say thank you. Jane said, "The blessings received from these three geese and now from the one remaining have been too numerous to count. Last fall I was alone for a week while Jerry went to DC on an Honor Flight. A few days before Jerry left, a mountain lion appeared very near the house. I had to go out to feed the animals morning and night, and it was a great comfort to me to have Grace follow me all over the yard; somehow, I knew she would take care of me."

Seems to me the geese taught Jane and Jerry a valuable lesson about the secret life of animals and their ability to sense things.

Jane closed with this: "Grace returned only one time after she spent the time with me while Jerry was gone. She disappeared shortly after he returned and many months later on a cold, wintry day she appeared, ate like she had not eaten for weeks, and then disappeared and has not been seen since. We think her grandgeese return to the pond, as they are not too leery of us, so maybe we are seeing her descendants now."

I've no doubt you are, Jane—none at all.

There are other feathered friends who have engaged in strange, seemingly unbelievable actions. Take the turkeys seen in a viral video posted on YouTube by *Inside Edition* and others that shows about fifteen turkeys walking in a circle around a cat that was lying dead in a roadway. What was this seemingly ritualistic behavior of a flock of turkeys? Was it a soul send-off for the cat's energy? That is the direction my thoughts take. Granted, it could be many things. I listen to my voice from inside and make my own mind up. It hasn't led me wrong yet.

Jane and Jerry were not finished telling me stories about their interaction with other feathered friends. They relayed a story about some white doves (actually white racing pigeons) they owned and rented out to people for weddings and funerals.

These birds are taught from an early age to return to their home when released at an event. On three occasions, things didn't quite happen as they usually did. Jane said, "After a release, one pigeon would not immediately follow the others home but would circle back around as if to check on the mourners and make sure they were all right. At one funeral at a Catholic Church in Helena, Montana, one circled back, perched on the steeple of the church, and watched the mourners from this perch for at least a minute if not more. It then followed its mates home."

One release was for a young woman killed in a car accident. Her family was holding a memorial service on the day that should have been her wedding day. The doves were released by several family members, and again, one came back and circled before joining the others. The birds are taught to head right home and are very hungry at the time of release. It is normal for them to head home as soon as possible, and it was unusual to have one hold back. This did not happen at the releases at the weddings but seemed to happen at funerals.

They took the doves to the wedding of a young Marine, and the doves were released by the wedding couple and members of the families. The doves zoomed out and headed for home. Eleven months later they took the doves to the same young Marine's funeral. He had been killed while on active duty in Afghanistan. The service was held at his family ranch outside of Helena. Once again, the doves were released by family members, and once again, one came back and circled around the gathering and then joined the others to head home. Coincidence? I don't know, but each time it left everyone breathless.

You know me, and you know that I do not put much stock in coincidence, leaning instead to a strong belief in the powers of this universe. In my world, the bird was directed back to the mourners by the energy of the recently deceased for one last bit of peace, belief, and a redirect of thought from pain and longing to one of amazement at the magic of the moment.

I have many friends in Canada, and this is a story about one of them. Mitzy Tait-Zeller lives in Swift Current, Saskatchewan. She is a lifelong horseperson and makes her living taking care of other people's horses as an equine balanced hoof trimmer, which is just one of the many hats she wears. What she experienced tells me that we all are in for surprises in life if only we remain open and stop writing things off as coincidental.

We Need Each Other

MITZY STARTED THE STORY THIS way: "At 11:20 p.m. on a cold February night I went down to our attached garage to have one last smoke for the night. I had only been out for a minute or so when I heard one of my horses whinny. I continued to listen, and the same horse whinnied again. In the few minutes it took me to finish my cigarette, the horse had whinnied six times. I was alerted to this because it was not normal herd behavior for my horses. I couldn't easily identify which one of my horses was having the issue, but I figured I better go out and see if everything was okay. I put a few more layers of winter clothing on over my pajamas and turned the yard light on before I walked out into the twenty-below-zero night."

The yard light only extended its beams to the end of the barn; beyond that, it was pretty much pitch-black. It was one of those nights where the stars and moon were obscured by cloud cover, and this particular night it was eerily quiet because their stretch of the highway was closed due to a cargo cleanup about a mile south of them. She had to use the flashlight on her phone to even see where to walk through the corral and down the alley to the back pasture. Mitzy could hear one horse whinny again, and it seemed to be coming from down the fence line to the north.

She listened to the snow crunch under her boots as she walked the length of the alley to the opening for their big pasture west of the yard. When she got to the end of the alley, she shut her flashlight off and just listened. Turning back toward the yard, she noted the outline of the many tree rows illuminated by the yard light up by the house. It was incredibly quiet and peaceful that night. Mitzy listened intently for another full minute or more and couldn't hear anything. No more whinnying and no crunching snow anywhere in the trees or the nearest part of the pasture to her. She could barely make out the snow nearest to her and could only see blobs of the white stuff throughout the blackness of the prairie landscape.

Mitzy hollered into the black vastness of the night, "Orca, Destry, Xarrow, Yuma, Yazmine! Come on!"

She listened. Nothing. Still no sound in the black void of the cold winter's night. She called again. "Orca, Destry, Star, Zeva, Duchess! Come on!"

Two seconds of silence was followed by a far-off whinny. She instantly recognized the whinny of the lead mare of the herd, a tiny Morgan mare named Orca. The horse whinnied back to her in answer. Now she could hear the distant thunder of her herd of horses running toward her in the darkness as Orca whinnied a reply that they were coming.

Mitzy stood fast in the darkness that did not allow her to see past twenty feet of snow as fifteen horses ran at her in the night. It was both exhilarating and terrifying as she heard the thundering hoof beats rapidly approach her. Every hair on her arms and the back of her neck stood at attention as she breathed in fresh cold air, awaiting their rapid arrival. The narrow white blaze of Orca became visible only a short distance away as she broke stride to stop just a few feet from her. Several of the herd galloped up beside Orca as she greeted Mitzy. Orca stood there protectively shielding her from being pushed by any of the herd, but she allowed a few of them to greet her briefly before they filed up the narrow alley toward the barn and corral. Three horses were ahead of them as Orca and Mitzy walked up the alley side by side.

When they reached the corral and stepped into some light from the yard, she stopped and allowed Mitzy to wrap her arms around her neck for a hug. Orca reciprocated the hug by wrapping her head around Mitzy's body briefly before she went to the water trough for a drink. Mitzy stood there waiting for the remainder of the herd to come up into the corral; like all good stewards of animals, she had to account for each of her horses. Yuma, Dancer, Aries, Star, and Cayenne all stopped to give her a hug that night. It was a magical moment with her herd of horses. Once the entire herd had been accounted for and all the hugs gifted, Mitzy stood and admired them, sending them loving energy.

It was in that moment she remembered it had been nearly a week since she had been out to see her horses. Her husband had been feeding them during the cold spell, and she had been preoccupied with other things. Had they missed her? Did one of them call her wondering where she was? Until that night, she had never thought they might miss her presence.

Mitzy lingered a little longer in the dim light of the corral with her horses. She didn't have to walk anywhere. Each of them took turns coming to see her, smell her, or just stand with her, sharing the energy of their presence. Mitzy came to a new realization that night about the love and positive energy her herd of horses brought to her spirit. Not only did she need them for therapy, but they needed her too in a sense she hadn't realized before. Mitzy realized she was more than just a source of food for them; she was a friend as well as an integral part of their herd.

Mitzy's gift from the horses that night was an imparting of wisdom letting her know they missed her presence in their lives. They wanted to see her and sense if all was okay with her. Mitzy said, "After spending a lifetime with these beautiful animals, I know I am part of them and them me. In a herd setting, I am alpha, and they accept that with grace, and together, we are one. They light my path with love and peace, and they stand as guiding angels in this life of mine."

I have been gifted with glimpses of the possible and
have become a true believer that all things
can happen with hope, faith, and focus. Only you can see
your magic.

Things do not have to happen with the animal right in front of you. Sometimes, as I learned from Pam Cox of South Carolina, our companions can be gone and still send messages meant for us alone. We have all heard stories about pennies from heaven, where pennies magically appear in front of people with memorable dates, reflective of those who have passed on from our earthly confines. Or how about feathers appearing, seemingly floating from out of nowhere and gifted to us? Their appearance never fails to remind us of someone or something from another time in our lives. Well, this is one of those stories but with something other than a penny or feathers.

Messages from Beyond

S EVERAL YEARS AGO, BOTH OF Pam's geldings were humanely helped into the next world. Dakota, a sorrel saddlebred in his early twenties, had no physical problems until about a year earlier when he began to have a series of issues in his front hooves resulting in founder and a major rotation of his coffin bones. Her other horse Ranger, a chestnut blanket Appaloosa also in his early twenties, had many life-limiting problems of his own. He had a severe case of Cushing's disease plus both upper and lower ringbone, and both of these diseases were taking their toll. These two drew such energy from each other, and that energy allowed them to continue beyond what a horse on a lot by himself could have done. They were the truest of amigos. Once the decision was reached that the kindest thing Pam could do for Dakota was to let him cross the bridge to better things, she turned to Ranger and asked him what he wanted to do, and she felt a clearly received message he wanted to leave this world with his best buddy. The two of them had been together with no other horses for ten years. Before making the appointment with the veterinarian to have the euthanasia performed, she contacted an animal communicator for a reading. She

221

reported that Ranger said he was tired and wanted to leave with his friend. This was devastating to Pam but confirmed the message she had received from Ranger.

My heart goes out to Pam for having to face such an issue and make the best decision for all concerned. I have known many people over the years who have faced the same issue with their animals, and it is never easy. It is a time that will be guaranteed to be full of self-reflection for years afterward. We make the best decisions we can for our charges and then must live with the results of those decisions. The loneliness and panic that would have been felt by Ranger after being part of a team for more than a decade would have undoubtedly hastened his demise. So the question is, which is better? To allow him to go with his longtime friend from a place of comfort in the normal or after a death brought on from not just his health challenges but also fear, loneliness, and confusion? I know which I would elect to do. Just remember, judging is not our job; understanding and empathy is. As an aside, Pam later asked her animal communicator for messages from Ranger, and without prompting, she said, "He said his body was tired, and he wanted to stay with his buddy." And he thanked her for letting him go. That is confirmation enough for me.

About two years after that, one of Pam's best friends unfortunately succumbed to her many medical problems. She had also been her main animal communicator for many years, and both of her geldings had talked to her. In fact, Dakota would sometimes just drop in to chat. Her friend was rather eccentric and what some call New Age in many ways and followed her own path. She spent time casting runes, receiving energy from stones, and such. She also had a wonderfully developed sense of humor and a deep belief in a universal, loving God and guardian angels.

Several times after she passed, Pam had wondered if her geldings were two of the very many waiting for her friend on the other side of the rainbow bridge. Pam was sitting in the den one night focusing on this very thought. After some reflection, she got up to go into the garage to recycle a bottle and saw something on the back steps. She picked it up. It was an earring in the shape of a unicorn head with wings attached as though it were an angel. Pam knew then this was from her horses and her friend. She had no earrings like that, and no one had come through the back door in weeks except for Pam and her husband. There was no other explanation. A unicorn with wings would be in line with her friend's sense of humor. As Pam sat there, she said aloud, "They are together." And she heard a resounding *yes*, as though someone was shouting next to her. Pam felt a weight lift off her shoulders and a warm, loving energy all around her.

Pam closed with this thought: "I know this sounds surreal. But it did happen."

Pam, I have not one single grain of doubt that things occurred just as you described, as I too have witnessed many magical events while observing the lives of the animals around us. Some may not believe, but I am not among them. Journey on, fellow traveler, and may you see many more things that will validate your beliefs. I know that is my life plan.

> Once you master the mindset that we are
> immortal souls having a physical experience,
> you learn how free you truly are.

Now let us visit with Joanne, who hailed at the time from a small town in the middle of Michigan, a small agricultural community between Lansing and Detroit. Her story adds weight to the idea that animals can communicate with you even if they are not in close proximity.

Breeze

JOANNE TOLD ME, "I GREW up on my horse Breeze. She was half quarter horse and half Arab. She was a stunning buckskin. When she was born, a wolf pack visited her home and attacked. By the time the owners came out with guns blazing, her mother had lost her fight, and Breeze became an orphan. I met her when she was only one year old. I was also an orphan, so I felt we had an immediate connection. My mother left us when I was around five years old, and I lived with an abusive stepmother until I was twelve when my brother and I ran away to successfully rejoin our birth mother."

Breeze would do anything for Joanne. Once she jumped a creek that she knew was too deep and too wide. But she jumped right in anyway, and under they both went. Joanne slid off and swam to the other side. Breeze turned around and climbed the bank on the side they had come from and turned to look at Joanne with a look that said, "That didn't work out." Joanne stood on the other side of the creek, with hands in the air and asked, "Why are you over there? Damn it!" Finally, she had to jump back into the murky waters and swim to her. Breeze never left even though they were home and the barn wasn't far. She stood there waiting for Joanne to get back on.

One day, Joanne decided to run Breeze along a manmade creek with dirt piles left along the sides. Eventually, grass and weeds had grown up, and it was difficult to tell where there was a mound of dirt or just how big it was. But Joanne thought it would be fun to ride and jump the mounds as fast as they could. Breeze stumbled, and Joanne flew over Breeze's head. Joanne hit the ground, landing straight on her back, and had the wind knocked out of her lungs. She remembers the sky being a beautiful summer-day blue with big, white, fluffy, cotton clouds. As she lay there gasping for air, she felt a nuzzle on her shoulder and put her hand up to touch Breeze's nose.

"I'm okay. It's okay. I'm sorry. It's okay," Joanne said to her.

Breeze stood and waited for her to catch her breath and climb back on.

Joanne's mom sold Breeze when she was fourteen. She was devastated, angry, and confused. The only constantly positive thing in her life had been Breeze. Then one night after Breeze had left, she woke her—and Joanne means her presence actually woke her; it was not a dream.

Joanne saw bright lights and heard Breeze neigh. Joanne knew she was trying to find her. She didn't know where she was, but she knew she was hurt badly. Joanne cried, prayed, and apologized. Then she heard her sister's truck start. She was a local vet tech and was on call that night. Joanne knew in her heart where she was going and what she was going to have to do. She was paralyzed. She wished she could have moved, but she couldn't. Joanne lay there in bed, crying and praying and telling Breeze help was on the way. It was going to be okay. She felt it wasn't going to be okay but said the words anyway.

Breeze had been hit by a truck, and her sister later told her it was a "horrible scene" and it was better that she didn't jump in her truck and go with her. Joanne still cries every time she thinks of Breeze. She strongly felt this was not how their relationship was supposed to end.

Joanne had many great adventures with that little mare. She said, "Breeze would race anything; a ten-speed downhill with mailboxes in our way, a dirt bike, a thoroughbred ... and she always gave her all, leaving them in the dust. Nothing new ever phased her. She was confident I would take care of her, and I was confident that she'd never leave me. In the end, though, I felt I abandoned her, and it has had a lifetime effect on me."

Even though Joanne's emotions are still raw after thirty-eight years of carrying them around, she still has a lifetime of loving memories to carry with her. The connection she shared with Breeze was extremely powerful. For Breeze to awaken her in her time of desperate need is testament to that connection. Folks, this was not a dream. This was sleeping one minute and wide awake, bathed in light the next and knowing without doubt her old friend was in need of her help. Breeze wanted her to know she was trying to find her—to find her way home. Nothing else can explain what happened.

It is Joanne's belief that every little girl deserves to be loved by a horse because of the strength of the love she felt when in the presence of Breeze and the unconditional love Breeze sent to her. She wishes more people could share the experience and witness the love. She also wishes she had recognized the depth of Breeze's love and had reciprocated in kind more than she felt she did. I will say this: after many conversations with Joanne about this story, I feel Breeze knew exactly how much she was loved, and she sent that same level of love back to Joanne.

The following is an excerpt from a short story Joanne wrote about Breeze when she was a thirteen-year-old eighth grader:

> As I ride atop of my horse Breeze, along the left side of a familiar gravel road, I gaze up at the sky. A clear blue sky with no signs of clouds and a blazing sun off to my left ... On my right, there is a ditch of trees,

brush, and weeds, with another corn field beyond. It's mid-September, and the corn is nearing harvest.

As I gather up the reins, I feel the familiar twinge of excitement in my stomach. I lean forward, scratching where the mane grows out of Breeze's neck. Her ears twitch as she pushes her nose forward, as if to check the tension of the reins. I rub both sides of her neck before grasping around to help me maintain my balance when she takes off. As I tighten my grip, I squeeze my lower heels into Breezes sides and we're off!

I think memories, like life's lessons, are written on the shells of our souls, as if etched with a hammer and chisel by some celestial master engraver. They remain forever a part of all we are and guide our decisions for eternity.

Dreamers are always welcome here.

For this encounter, we take a trip back in time to a much earlier era, a time of growth in the new west. The story comes to us from a very spry eighty-two-year-young Barbara Rentner who hails from Lynnwood, Washington. She is proud of every one of those eighty-two years and will tell you so. It was a story told to her as a small child by her grandfather, Oscar. Oscar was described as a man of few words and was a tough little guy of Scot and Irish ancestry. He had left his home as a thirteen-year-old and started his life by going to work for the railroad, selling newspapers and candy before working his way up to brakeman and later conductor and retiring at seventy-two as a baggage handler. He lost a finger to a coupler but never his heart for working the rails. He was a spry banty rooster to the end.

It was at this point, while listening to the teller of the tale, that I traveled back in time to my own early youth. I could vividly remember sitting on the old couch with my father, listening to him tell me of his growing up in rural Georgia on a farm. There were many stories about horses, mules, and his favorite dog, Biff, an American bulldog. I can still smell his Old Spice aftershave and the cigar he constantly had in the corner of his mouth, and I remember each story as if it were told today. Those memories are some of my proudest possessions.

As I read Barbara's story, I could envision her sitting on her grandfather's lap, feeling safe as his gnarled and misshapen hands gently supported her as he spoke of long-ago times. Maybe the night was cold and the light came from oil lanterns, while the warmth radiated from a crackling fire in a potbellied stove. Caught up in the cadence of his voice, her head rested on his shoulder, and her mind created images to accompany the words he spoke.

Great Gobben

OSCAR TOLD THE STORY OF his family's horse, Great Gobben, and life in early Nova Scotia. The horse was a do-everything horse of unknown heritage. He could pull a buggy or be saddled for transportation, but before one particular night, they had no idea of the depth of his intuition.

On the day of the story, it was stormy with off-and-on showers. Regardless of the rain, supplies were needed, so Gobben was hitched to the one-horse wagon. Oscar, his mother, and another relative whose name is lost to the winds, loaded up, braved the storms, and made their way across the mountain divide to town. Oscar was but a ten-year-old boy at the time.

The trip was initially uneventful; it wasn't until the return trip home that things took an unexpected turn. It was already dark, and the way was lit by what little ambient light was available and the lanterns mounted on the front corners of the wagon. As they approached a bridge over a river divide, Gobben came to a complete stop. No one cued him to halt; he did it on his own and refused to go forward. No amount of coaxing would change his mind.

The unnamed relative got out of the wagon and took a whip to Gobben, trying to get him to go forward, but he wouldn't budge. Use of a whip was a sign of the time where we trained and coaxed through dominance and pain instead of through asking and understanding. Oscar exited the wagon and tried to gently guide Gobben by tugging on his bridle. Nothing was going to work. Oscar's mother gave up and turned the wagon around, deciding not to go farther in the darkness. They ended up staying with a friend in town who also put Gobben up for the night.

The next day dawned bright and sunny—one of those days without a cloud in sight and the sky a surreal blue. Everyone's attitude brightened with the sun's rays and warmth. They hitched Gobben up to the wagon and started for home once again. As they approached the bridge, they saw a crowd and heard people talking excitedly. Drawing closer to the bridge head, they saw a sign had been posted sometime after their encounter the night before with a warning: "Do not cross. Bridge out." The bridge had fallen into the water below.

All three of them looked at the sign and then at each other, and they knew without doubt Gobben had saved their lives the night before. His refusal to cross the bridge saved himself and his three charges. Needless to say, Gobben was viewed in a different light the rest of his days, and the whip was retired. How he knew the bridge was out is a question for the ages. I just know that since cancer came to visit me, I have looked at the world through a different lens. I no longer see coincidence, and I no longer look to science for all answers. I view this world as one full of possibilities and innumerable synchronicities where anything can happen.

A few years later, Gobben had another brush with the supernatural, and Oscar was there once again to see what happened. Oscar was with his father in the wagon with Gobben at the lead. They were deep in the forest on a two-track wagon road with the trees close on each side. All of a sudden, he once again came to a complete stop in the middle of the road and couldn't be coaxed to move forward. By this time, they had learned to allow him his visions.

It wasn't long before a green mist arose from the ground and slowly grew to a man-sized cloud. It hung in the air for a couple of minutes, undulating in the sky before rapidly dissipating. Without cue, as soon as the mist disappeared, Gobben picked up where he left off and continued the journey. What was the mist? How did Gobben know it was going to appear? Why didn't he spook when it did? Those are questions without answers for now. As I am told repeatedly, this will all make sense someday.

The elderly of this country are the keepers of our history. They are full of tales, some absolute truth and some slightly embellished. The subject of each tale carries the full weight of truth with it because behind each stretch of fact lies the truth that birthed the story to begin with.

Those stories only stay alive as long as the teller's breath flows unless you pick up and carry the legacy forward. Talk to your relatives, make notes, or, better yet, record their words. Nothing quite captures our imagination like sitting next to a parent or grandparent and hearing a tale in his or her voice. Keep your family's history alive for other generations. Return the elderly to a place of importance and respect. They have earned the seat. My thanks to Barbara Rentner for sharing her family's tales with us.

Life is change; growth is choice.

One of the good things about social media is the reconnecting with old friends we might not have seen in decades. That is the case with John Beisel. We grew up in the same area and went to the same schools. Our early lives were mirror images of life at the time. He came from a family with six siblings (all girls) and I with four. We dealt with the same challenges of growing up without enough money for more than the basics, but luckily, we didn't know we might not have what others took for granted until much later in life.

As is often the case, after graduation from high school, I never saw or talked to John again until 2017 when we reconnected via social media. I did find out that his background was in education. His educational accomplishments are many, honorable, and diverse. He taught for the Owensboro Kentucky Public School system and Henderson Community College and has been involved in educational matters not only on the state level but nationally.

We hit the ground running and found out that our lives had some amazing synchronicities, even to the point of having the same hobbies in reading, photography, and woodworking. We have had the opportunity to meet in person over coffee and memories and will again. I think maybe most importantly, we were blessed to have seen the depth of the animal kingdom that most people miss. His vision led to the penning of the below story. I found the depth of his insight inspiring and his ability to tell a tale missing nothing but a campfire, some sipping whiskey, and a log to prop your feet on. Sit back, and enjoy. You might just learn that the universe is trying to teach us, if only we are willing to learn.

John's Story

I do not understand the human race.
It has so little love for creatures with a different face.
Treating animals like people is no madness or disgrace.
I do not understand the human race.

— Dr. Doolittle

"I WAS FORTUNATE TO GROW UP in the country. The community of farmers provided me with an opportunity to develop a work ethic. They also incentivized my efforts to work with my mind instead of my back. More importantly, I was exposed to life—the good, the bad, the serious, and the hilarious.

Dad raised basset hounds, and at one time we had twenty-seven dogs in three pens. A cricket couldn't pass gas without everyone in the surrounding area knowing about it. We all slept soundly knowing no one could approach the house without setting off the alarm. Once when the dogs sounded off, dad slipped out, hid under the porch, and tensely waited. He banged his head on the porch floor when the collie ran his tongue into dad's ear. The lesson here is watch out for the collie.

We were able to keep a menagerie of animals, both feral and domestic. I was exposed to the birth of puppies at an early age and before that the breeding. Sex and the results were not a mystery; it was simply life. Death, however, remained elusive.

We had an AKC-registered champion named Lulu, and she was the smartest hunter I knew. Her relentless pursuit of game often found Dad's field jacket lying on the ground with us heading to the house. The next morning would find her curled up on the jacket ready to go home.

I was about five years old when I went to the outbuilding where we had a whelping box for her pups. The building was warm so we opened the door and attached her to a length of chain so she could get some fresh air. The pups were old enough to leave the box, and the runt, Tiny, was suspended off the floor with the chain wrapped around his neck. I wasn't strong enough to pull Lulu back to release the chain, so I ran to the house for Mom. Mom ran to the shed, but it was too late for Tiny. I placed him in a metal lunch box, and Dad buried him under a walnut tree and made a concrete stone commemorating him. I had been part of butchering animals and have lost animals since, but Tiny's death still haunts me.

I was a frequent visitor to Lulu and her pups subsequent to that event. On one occasion, she was lying in the shade nursing her pups.

As I petted her head, she turned and looked into my soul. With the sad eyes of a basset looking at me, I saw deeper. I realized, at five, there was much more to growth than breeding and birth. She knew to take care of her pups; she had to feed, protect, and teach her pups. She knew life was hard work, and at the time, I thought she failed. But now I know the Grand Creator set up Tiny's sacrifice to provide a lesson for me. I cannot give you that lesson; it is an unspoken message that cannot be articulated.

Continuing the lessons, I learned early in life, here is the story about Bub and Maynard. A beautiful calico cat showed up one day, as did many feral animals or ones that someone abandoned. We didn't know she came with a family until she brought one female and three male kittens to the house. *The Many Loves of Dobie Gillis* provided the names Dobie, Chatsworth, Zelda, and, of course, Maynard G. Krebs. Maynard was black and white, I assume courtesy of his dad, with a patch of black on his chin. The others went their own ways, but Maynard hung around for a long, albeit lazy, life.

Bub was a red-dyed Easter chick. Although now we recognize the cruelty of dyeing chicks, at the time, we thought it was neat. Bub was playful and would hop up in any lap for a visit, particularly with my younger sister who claimed ownership. Maynard exuded the personality of his television namesake, somewhat of an Alfred E. Newman, "What? Me worry?" attitude. He would tolerate petting and nuzzling but didn't seek it. We kept a bed on the front porch for him. It was on the north side of the house generally sheltered from storm and always shaded.

Bub and Maynard shared that bed, and it taught me that although wild animals do kill for food, they aren't necessarily natural enemies. Just because someone looks or thinks different than me doesn't imply that they should be shunned or attacked. If my needs are sufficiently met, why can't I share with the less fortunate?

The lessons from animals continued throughout my life. We tried to raise rabbits, but unbeknownst to us, we had two bucks. I do believe that life is the most powerful force in this world. Left alone, life will consume. Abandoned cabins, old boats, sunken ships, and old air strips soon find that time has covered them with life, be it weeds, worms, algae, or grass. The need to procreate is the driving force in this speck of dirt we call home. Those poor buck rabbits! Try as they might, they weren't going to make bunnies. They took turns in their attempts, but the only thing they produced was laughter on my part and another valuable lesson. Thoughts on homosexual rabbits will follow.

We had hogs, banty chickens, crows, groundhogs, turtles, snakes, and one sorry-a## turkey in our menagerie. He was a mean-spirited bird who would attack an anvil given the chance. I cannot say I was unhappy when he choked on a piece of string. He may be the source of my aversion to mean-spirited people. Lesson learned.

We had a half dozen banty chickens and one rooster. The rooster was aggressive to other animals, although he never caused me problems. His demise, I think, was the result of combat with a fox. Regardless, the hens were without a rooster. One brown speckled hen transformed herself in a way I still have trouble understanding. I understand the purpose of the transformation but not how it was accomplished. Over the course of a few months, she grew a small comb and proceeded to substitute for the missing cock. We had a grape arbor with short, four-foot posts suspending the wire for the grapes to climb. The hen, replete with comb, would fly up to the post and attempt to crow. I say *attempt* because her voice was scratchy and far from the normal crowing. Dad and I had many laughs at her attempt to fulfill the rooster's job. Try as she might, like the buck rabbits, she was not going to reproduce with the hens. I wrote a graduate paper on segments of society and included a dialogue about the rabbits and the hen. A discussion ensued as to whether she would be transgender or a transvestite. I argued because a physical change occurred, she would qualify as transgender. Homosexual rabbits and transgender chickens brought humor to the country and opened my eyes to other possibilities.

I am completely comfortable with my heterosexual male identity. From my perspective, transgender and homosexuality do not conform to Mother Nature's goal of procreation. From a procreative standpoint, those are aberrations. However, Ma Nature is a lot smarter than I am, and who am I to judge her accommodations? Does it matter if you're LGBTQIA or XYZ? As an old psychology professor used to say, "You go to hell your way, and I'll go to hell mine." I guess time has taught me to sleep with the cat and rooster.

Time: Now there's an enigma of epic proportion. Time allows young bucks to become old fools, unless you keep your eyes on the animals.

My daughter picked up a Carolina dog from the animal shelter. The Carolina was a feral breed in the swamps of North and South Carolina. Discovered by archeologists and domesticated in the 1980s, they are sometimes referred to as the American dingo. My daughter said the dog wasn't a full Carolina but rather mixed. Although I never asked, what is a full-bred feral? Soon after she acquired the pup, she and her then husband went on a two-week vacation. Raoul spent those two weeks with me, and we bonded. He recognized me as an alpha and still does. His greeting always included licking around my lips, a sign of welcome back. I saw that same behavior when visited by the man who cared for him at the shelter. I've seen him take my ex-wife's hand very gently and lead her around with an I'm-in-charge attitude and then release her. He T-boned a German shepherd just to establish dominance. His eighty pounds took down a 120-pound Newfoundland until she stopped wiggling, and then he let her up. I saw two neighborhood dogs literally bow down in his presence absent any barking or growling from him. I may have been his alpha, but he was second in command. There are shades of white around my old friend's muzzle now. He doesn't move as fast as he once did, and getting up is a bit more of a chore.

One evening he was lying on his bed while I was watching television. I don't sneeze often, but when I do, it is generally strong. I sneezed, and Raoul jumped up faster than I had seen in a while, came to the couch, and straddled my thighs. His nose was about six inches from mine, his ears laid back, and his tail motionless. His head didn't move, but his eyes darted from side to side trying to decide if I was okay. After a few minutes, he licked my mouth, dismounted the couch, and returned to his bed. It was two old men, lifelong friends checking on each other.

Another lesson for all of us: How much does it take to utter the four words "How are you today?" and mean it?

God does, in fact, move in mysterious ways. I stopped hearing His voice from the pulpit but never doubted His presence in my life. He speaks to me through mathematics and physics. It took me a number of years to realize His lessons from my furry friends.

I didn't hear a single dog, cat, or chicken condemning the rabbits. Not a single animal said the cat can't sleep with the chicken. There was not a sound bemoaning the hen for her crowing. Maybe we should listen to the animals, and particularly listen for the absence of negative rhetoric.

"In God we trust. Everybody else has to pay cash. If we cannot rid ourselves of the animus lurking in our hearts, the cost will be mighty," John Beisel said. "To avoid this mighty cost, maybe it is time for us to understand that what we think is the truth is just something we were taught by those who thought they knew. This is a much more magical place than I ever envisioned while growing into a man, and I am glad to have arrived where I am. My new place is one of infinite possibilities."

How else do you explain John's observations? Let's add one more to the mix.

Dr. Wayne Dyer chronicled an event that happened in South Africa during March 2012 and involved world-renowned elephant rescuer and rehabilitator, Lawrence Anthony. Lawrence spent his life championing the lives of elephants all over the world. Mr. Anthony died March 7, 2012, at his farm, leaving behind his family and scores of other people he touched during his stay here.

Two days after his passing, thirty-one elephants led by two matriarchs arrived at Lawrence's home after a twelve-mile, single-file march. They arrived without prompting by any human. The elephants appeared to be solely focused upon paying their respects to the person who saved their lives. Keep in mind, they had not been to this farm in more than three years. They stayed for two days and nights without food or water, and as slowly as they walked in, they left to walk home. They showed their love and respect for a human who made sure they had a safe place to exist. There is simply no other way to explain their action.

How did they know? How indeed! Is there a possibility that we do not know quite what we think we know about the ways of the universe? I think that is the case. Perhaps Dr. Dyer said it best when he said, "Something in the universe is greater and deeper than human intelligence."

Learn from the John Beisels and the Wayne Dyers of this world. Things are much deeper than we have been previously taught. There is magic afoot, be open and be part of it.

> If we counted our friends as often as we
> counted our money, we would realize how
> rich we are in things that matter most.

If you are like me, you have gone through life thinking you had it all figured out. You knew what was real and what was woo-woo. If you are lucky, like I was, you got to go through an awakening and discover what is really hidden just out of sight. These discoveries usually come on the heels of a major life challenge—one that makes you reconsider all you thought you knew.

You may mistakenly think you are the only one to have such eye-opening experiences, but the good thing about enlightenment, growth, and discovery is you want to share your experiences with others, so eventually you share your stories and observations freely. This sharing and the resulting feedback are where you discover the ways this universe is connected.

Just as I met a horse that tried to convince me that we knew each other on another level, so did Lisa Broughton, the owner of Turquoise Horse Ranch in Gainesville, Texas.

Quintaesencia

IT WAS THE FALL OF 1999 in Texas, a brown fall that arrived on the heels of a hot, dry Texas summer. Lisa's daughter Jenna was ready to start taking horseback riding lessons, and Lisa was excited for her. They are a horse family from a long line of horse families, and the lessons were preordained. It was time.

Lisa had done her homework and made a decision about who would be the one to teach her daughter. Bill Harwood rose to the top of the list and was highly recommended. He had been an Arabian horse trainer for years and was from the close by community of Flower Mound.

During their first visit to his ranch, Lisa said, "we drove slowly up Bill's driveway, just looking at all the Arabians. Oh my gosh, their heads were so gorgeous, their eyes looked shiny and black with black skin around the eye, their tails curled over their backs as they ran. It was almost a challenge to drive up the driveway as the horses possessed a certain kind of magic you could feel; I could hardly keep my eyes on the road."

When they stopped and stepped out of their car, Lisa noticed a horse loudly whinnying and running toward her across the pasture. She initially thought it was odd and that maybe it was feeding time. Lisa and Jenna got busy meeting Bill and proceeding with what would be the first of many lessons and planting seeds of friendship for the future.

The fall slowly turned into winter, and the weather wasn't exactly conducive to lessons outside, so Bill moved things inside the barn into a round pen. Lisa wisely understood it was better for her not to be present when her daughter's lessons were going on, so she would step out of sight and wait for the lesson to end as she watched the other horses moving about.

Lisa's second meeting with the horse that acted a bit odd on that first day took place behind the scenes. Of the second meeting, Lisa said, "I waited near the wash stall and watched the horses come into the barn. One of the barn grooms who was bringing the horses in had a beautiful paint horse he was leading. This horse stopped dead square in front of me and started nickering at me. I just sat there and thought, *This is the same horse that was running up the fence and whinnying at me quite feverishly on the first day!* I asked the groom what the mare's name was. He replied that her name was Tess. I asked the groom if she always talked to people. He said no and gave a hard yank on the lead rope to take her back to her stall. She was such a sight to see, so beautiful, and she was talking to me! I found out later from Bill that Tess was a registered half Arabian and half pinto, and her registered name was Quintaesencia. Now, I was mesmerized and could not stop thinking about this magical mare!"

Every time Jenna had a lesson, Lisa would drop her off and make tracks for Tess's stall for a visit and a talk. Lisa, like me, believes in sitting down and having conversations with animals. Try it sometime; their reaction might just surprise you. From Bill, Lisa found out that Tess's owner's name was Beth, and it was apparent that Lisa and she were not at the ranch on the same days. Eventually, Lisa and Beth met, but before that, Bill noticed Lisa had taken a liking to Tess, and one day he asked her if she would like to ride the mare. Lisa answered with a resounding, "Me? Really?" Bill let her know he had already cleared it with Beth who had heard of the developing connection between her horse and Lisa.

Here is Lisa's recollection of that first ride: "From the moment I got on Tess's back, it was like two beings becoming one. We galloped across the pen pell-mell, and there was a puddle of water. Her owner was there watching us fly around, and Beth yelled, 'Don't take her near the water, or she will spook.' We ran pell-mell through the water, and we (Tess and I) laughed. She laughed inside, and I had tears rolling down my face from joy. How do you know a horse is laughing? Because her body vibration changed, and it was joyous; she was enjoying herself. Stride after stride, we ran in circles across the water, ignoring Beth's concerns. When we finished riding, there was mud all over Tess's white legs, and I likened our behavior to four-wheeling at a dressage barn. She was able to be a horse. It was the first day of many years to come."

In December 2001, Beth asked Lisa if she wanted to buy Tess, and Lisa answered with an immediate and unquestionable yes. The day of the sale, dressage was over for Tess, and she was on her way to being a trail horse. All because, on some level, Tess knew Lisa's soul from someplace else and made sure Lisa knew that she knew. The reunion was complete, and the rest of their lives were about to begin.

There was a lot of learning to go through initially. Unknown to Lisa, Tess had never been a trail horse. As a matter of fact, she had never been ridden outside a ring. Lisa said, "Believe it or not, it never occurred to me that Tess had never ridden on an equestrian trail. I mean, she was a horse. Don't all horses trail ride? Not so. The mare was ridden only inside the riding arena at Bill's old place. Our first trail ride, unbeknownst to me, was Tess's maiden voyage, and she was quite skittish or, as the cowboys call it, *boogery*. We jumped and darted even at the sight of butterflies. I could not figure out what was going on. After all, I had owned the mare for quite some time at this point."

This is where things might get a little weird to the uninitiated, but to those of us who have glimpsed the truth hidden behind the curtain, it is so beautifully real. It happened on another of those days when Tess and Lisa were on a trail, and Tess was being what was interpreted as obstinate and frustratingly hardheaded. What Lisa finally noticed was this behavior always occurred at the same place adjacent to the woods, and that was her aha moment.

That was when Lisa decided to just sit right where she was in the saddle and connect to everything the only way she knew well, and that was through meditation. Lisa shared what happened with these words:

> The sun's rays were warming my face, and there was a summer breeze gently blowing. I would take a slow breath, and I would breathe in and out and feel my whole body becoming less tense and more relaxed. I drifted off for close to thirty minutes. I woke up still in the same place on Tess's back, and we had not moved one inch. It was as though she knew the whole time I needed to connect with nature.
>
> During my meditation, I saw white sparkles of lights, and I could hear them as they came to me as fairies; they said, "Thank you for cleaning up the trail." Then there was a woman in spirit named Alaya

who was a Native American who came up to Tess and myself while I was in meditation. She said that she was a watcher of the woods, and the woods know me and my mare. The forests as a whole are all vibrationally connected in consciousness. Because of this connection to all beings, the woods tell the stories from present to past. Alaya showed me the Divine white light of the trees and the creek that runs through the equestrian trail. It was as though I was being shown the energy and life of the forest. It felt as though it was an education for my care and my future endeavors. As I awakened from my meditation, Tess just stood there as still as could be, and she then began to walk forward without any hesitation. It was as though she was the one who wanted me to connect with the woods. It was just the beginning of my journey. Tess was my most excellent teacher, and she was the gatekeeper who opened the spiritual doors for me to see where I was previously asleep.

Amazingly, from the day of the meditation onward, Tess never once acted up again. It was if she had a lesson to teach, and nothing would stop her from passing it on to Lisa. Once taught, forever could begin.

Tess went on to be Lisa's first choice, and together they made a striking pair. Tess opened doors during their time together that Lisa didn't even know existed. Tess became an excellent trail horse, taking the lead on most rides. She was an exceptional communicator, even to the point of letting Lisa know she wanted to have a baby. And yes, Lisa made sure that happened. Tess has been on numerous campouts and travels annually to Arizona to ride in the Saguaro National Park with Lisa's parents, who are also avid riders.

Twenty-eight-year-old Tess has turned into the perfect lifetime horse, and nothing in this world can separate these two. Tess saw Lisa, recognized her soul, and knew what she had to do to convince Lisa to take her home where she belonged, and home with Lisa is where she will stay.

As has always been my nature, I seem to gravitate toward animal rescues of all kinds, and that habit brings me in touch with some of the warmest and most loving people on this planet. I was lucky enough one day to meet not only a special horse named Will but also the caring souls who take care of him when I went to the Downeast Equine and Large Animal Society (DELAS) located in Deblois, Maine, for a fundraiser. I was signing books and donating a portion of the proceeds to the rescue. The rescue is owned and operated by Debbie McLain and her husband, Junior. Debbie is a lifelong horseperson. She received her first horse at three years old but has been around them since birth. Junior came into horses via his marriage to Debbie and embraced them totally.

The Beauty of Will

WILL, A TWENTY-YEAR-OLD BLACK-AND-WHITE PAINT horse, had lived at the rescue for the past twelve years. You might think upon seeing Will that the first thing I would have noticed was his deformed nose, but the first thing I saw was Will's eyes. He had the most kind and soft eyes I have ever seen, and looking at them leaves you feeling at peace. It is almost as if he possessed an energy that drew you into the depths of his soul through his liquid, brown eyes. I knew right away this was a special horse, and I wanted to know his story.

When Debbie met Will, he was extremely underweight with ribs and hip points showing prominently but not emaciated to the point of overshadowing the power of his eyes or outweighing his potential. After weeks of negotiating with the owners, she agreed to take Will and another horse and provide their care until they could be rehomed.

Debbie said this about her first contact with Will: "We had been asked several times to take a couple of horses. Both were decent horses and very adoptable. Babe was a retired racehorse who had legs that needed to be watched and would only make a trail horse. Will was a black-and-white paint with a crooked nose. It didn't bother him, and it didn't affect his ability to eat or breathe, so it didn't bother us."

Debbie studied Will's condition in order to learn how to better take care of him and see if there was anything she should do differently. Will was born with a genetic congenital defect called wry nose. This defect develops in utero. The foal is born with a dramatic visual defect. Most horses born with wry nose are euthanized at birth. In some, the defect inhibits breathing and eating. Their nostrils can be occluded, and their teeth can be offset to the point of not being able to chew. That was not the problem with Will. Although he did snore, he did not experience any other breathing or eating problems. Debbie could see beyond the deformity. She knew that if the problem did not cause any quality-of-life issues, then he needed to be allowed to live his life simply as a horse and be treated the same as other horses.

Will was destined to spend his whole life at the rescue. He had been adopted twice but returned through no fault of his own. One couple went through a divorce, and the other couple lost their jobs. Debbie will not put a horse through more than two adoptions. I agree with her when she says that it hurts the horses to think they are at a forever home only to go back where they lived before, and she does not like seeing a lack of light in their eyes. She wants them to have continuity and a sense of belonging in their lives.

If you looked beyond Will's deformity, you would find a horse that was extremely calm. I have heard horses called bombproof but personally do not believe one exists. However, Will was about as close as you can get. He was ridden on a regular basis by people ranging from two to seventy. He treated everyone he met with respect, kindness, and a deep sense of calm, but he paid particular attention to people who were afraid of him.

Nothing fazed Will. Anybody could handle and ride him. He gave many first rides and taught many the joy of horses. Maybe it was because of his crooked face, but children gravitated to Will. Debbie and Junior never allowed anyone to tease Will or make fun of him. That crooked nose led to a heart of absolute gold. Will loved kids and would follow them around for hours just to be close to them. Many times, you could see Will standing with his head hanging to a child while the child jabbered at him. He probably heard more stories than the parents did. Debbie was betting he listened better too.

Each year they took some horses to a local trail-riding facility and had a fun day of riding and visitors. There was a young lady who had always wanted to ride, so she climbed on. Even a small horse seems big the first time you get up on one. She was terrified and panicked. Every muscle clenched. She was crying uncontrollably. There were volunteers around them, so Debbie just kept an eye on them from a distance. Most horses in these circumstances would shift around and get upset. Not Will. Head hanging, standing perfectly still, Will went to sleep. When the young lady calmed enough to be lifted off, Will still stood there quietly. He earned his permanent place that day. Will went on to teach more kids how to handle horses and learn their basic care.

It seemed Will truly couldn't care less about what anyone thought of the way he looked. Will was not treated any differently by the other animals at the rescue. None of them seem to recognize he looked different than the other horses. Some people shunned him because of his looks, but it was a rare occurrence. Most, unfortunately, took a glance in his direction and quickly looked away. Maybe we could learn some important lessons from Will and the other animals at DELAS.

Maybe, just maybe, we put way too much emphasis on appearance and not enough on the heart that lies within us all. Maybe we need to blindfold ourselves to what is pleasing to the eye and seek what is pleasurable to the soul. Only then will we find our potential as a species.

I am glad I met Will and appreciate the lessons he taught me that day. He taught me coexistence between our species depends upon us seeing the beauty within and not being drawn to the blemishes that lie on the surface. Beauty, though visually pleasing, has nothing to do with a kind heart and a willing soul—nothing at all.

Will was in a perfect place. He lived free range on forty-four acres with twenty-three other equines, a few pigs, geese, oxen, dogs, a llama, and barn cats. He lived around others who saw him for the heart within and not the damaged package he lived inside of. Support those who speak for the ones without voice. It is our job as humans to care for the animals we have domesticated. They ask nothing of us but our presence.

Sadly, Will passed away in the latter part of 2018. I know from talking to the many people whose lives he touched that Will had a good life and possessed absolutely no fear for his coming transition. Over the fall, his age really started to show. But he was eating and moving around as usual for a horse in his late twenties. Debbie had always had an extra treat, and while appreciative, you could tell that he felt as though it was his due. All their regular volunteers and visitors always made a point of taking a moment just for Will. He loved the attention, and they all knew their time with him was limited now. As fall progressed and winter loomed, they wondered how he would handle the colder weather.

Every morning as soon as it got light enough to see, Debbie checked on the horses up across the field. One morning when she looked, Will was standing in the hay pile with Risha, another longtime resident. An hour later as she walked up to the barn, she saw Will lying in the hay with Risha's head resting on his neck. Risha is a bit of a snot and not the friendliest horse, so she thought it was odd he was standing that close. When she got closer, she saw that although he was lying in a normal resting position, Will's eyes were cloudy. Debbie spoke his name, and he blinked, so she knew he was still with her. His eyes drifted shut for the last time; he snuffled once and was gone.

Debbie was in awe as she actually watched a mist rise from Will's warm body as his spirit left him. This was not an exhalation of breath but something she had never seen before. It was as if a mist the size of his body rose in the air and slowly dissipated. Her eyes misted over as she realized he had gifted her with something magical.

Debbie said, "People say animals have no feelings and no soul. Will is proof that they have both. He had waited to say goodbye before he crossed the rainbow bridge." Her heart shattered that morning, and she will never forget that as much as Will meant to so many people, she meant just as much to him. He will always be remembered as the little horse with a crooked face that conquered souls and collected hearts.

I think you will agree with me when I say Debbie was given the gift of a glimpse behind the veil separating us from what is not only magical but also the truth that we go through life pretending not to see. Please see that this life and the connected energy inside it are bigger than we have been taught, and we are more powerful than you can imagine.

How beautiful it is to find someone
who asks for nothing but your company.

Final Thoughts

THIS IS THE CHAPTER I have been looking forward to. Having reached the end of the book, I now have a chance to clear up any misconceptions the book may have raised about this magical world that surrounds us. Hopefully, after reading about the things animals are capable of doing, it is a world that is clearer and more focused than it may have been before. But to this point, I haven't addressed a most important aspect of the animal kingdom. For lack of a better term, let's refer to it as the dark side of things.

I knew when I started this project, I couldn't write a book singing the praises of animals and writing about their incredible spiritual depth and evolution without addressing the dark side of animals. In my mind, it is impossible to do one without doing the other.

How do you on the one hand write of the boundless and exciting actions that supposedly dumb animals perform without explaining to the parents of a two-year-old who was mauled to death by a pack of dogs how it could happen with an evolved species? Or what about the ten-year-old girl who died after being kicked in the head by the family's trusted horse? How about the lady who rescued pit bulls, only to be killed by those she was trying to save?

Please know my heart breaks for those who have experienced the loss of a loved family member as a result of actions taken by animals, and nothing I can possibly say will assuage their pain. This pain is personal to them, and even though it may soften in time, it will never quite go away. And the pain shouldn't go away; I see it as a way of keeping that person's memory alive. The pain of longing will be surrounded by memories that evoke laughter and smiles later in life. The sad part concerning the questions I have brought up about the dark side is that they cannot be answered by me. Only time and transition will bring the answers forth. Oh, I could guess all day long, but guesses are all they would be.

For instance, animals share some of the same diseases humans experience. For example, older animals can experience dementia, and this would affect how they interact with humans. Strokes, mental decline, cancer, constant pain from sore, aging joints, and more might affect how they act toward humans. They generally adapt to changes much better than we do, but how many instances of bad behavior could be attributed to illness? Until we have all the answers, here are some things about the animal kingdom you might not know.

As a small aside, let me tell you a little about the adaptability of animals that have been challenged by declining health. As mentioned earlier in the book, my wife's horse Bo experienced such a challenge. Bo is her longtime do-everything horse. He is still a big, handsome foundation quarter horse. He was twenty-eight years old when one night, alone in his stall, he suffered a stroke. From the looks of his stall, his initial reaction was one of panic. A few things were torn up, and the next morning he was still unsure about this new world he lived in, but within twenty-four hours, he was as calm as he could be. The stroke affected his vision. He now has close-up vision in one eye and distance vision in the other. He adapted to his new circumstances within that twenty-four-hour period. He was able to navigate his pasture, even at a run. He can find his water, hay ring, and stall just like before, albeit a bit slower, but with the same confidence as before. How many human stroke victims have you seen who have been able to adapt and recover within twenty-four hours? Animals are simply better at it than we are because they do not react from fear other than their initial reaction to the affront. Something tells me they know of life's continuance after crossing over and do not fear it. Now who is more evolved?

I interviewed several people for this portion of the book, and the theme of their answers seemed to be very close to the same, person to person. For purposes of the book, I will focus on one particular interview I had with Dr. Bruce Lyle, who lives and practices veterinarian medicine in Aubrey, Texas. He is a longtime practitioner, having graduated from Texas A & M, class of 1991, and had been in business for twenty-six years when I talked to him in 2017. Dr. Lyle focuses mostly on the equine side of things, and most of his experiences come from those interactions.

Dr. Lyle started the conversation by saying, "There are mean people, and there are mean animals." He long ago saw the parallels between the two camps and noticed that there are few differences between the two. Kindness usually begets kindness, and evil typically begets evil, but sometimes you can be kind and receive meanness in return because that is simply the nature of the particular animal you are dealing with.

He also noticed working horses and human athletes share a commonality. There is a change in emotion when it is time for the animal to do what it was trained to do. Dr. Lyle said, "Look in the eye of a proathlete when it is game time, and you will easily see the focus they have on the upcoming event." He went on to say if you ever have the chance to watch a polo match, you should watch the horses just before the game starts, and you can't help but see the intense focus they exhibit. Horse athletes are no different from human athletes, and you will see that same look in their eyes when it is time to go to work. Dr. Lyle sees the similarities between our species. The only difference is the packaging we come in and the languages we speak. Keep in mind animals communicate with each other about life, just as humans do. We just don't seem to recognize their method of communication. Inability to recognize something does not mean it doesn't exist.

Why would some animals be angry and willing to strike out toward humans, even to the point of killing one of us? Maybe the better question would be, why would they not? Exactly what have we done to them collectively to cause some of them to harbor anger toward us?

I will start with the fact that most of us are omnivores. It is our nature to consume animals. The concern isn't so much that we do eat them; it's the way we treat them when it is time to kill them. Is our treatment of them humane? Many times, the answer is no. They die in a position of fear because of the way they are treated.

Please do not think I am not empathetic toward farmers who are tasked with feeding the world. I not only am one, but some of my truest friends are full-time farmers, and I feel their frustration and pain. I know all about how difficult the job is. I simply think we could be more humane in our treatment and harvesting of animals when it is time for their energy to transition, leaving the shell behind for us.

I think we might do better at this if we studied early Native Americans. Not only were they deeply spiritual in their everyday lives, but they believed in giving thanks to the animal and, yes, the plants for their very sustenance. This may seem odd to some of us. The Native American people only killed what they could eat without spoilage. The braves were tasked with hunting and the women with gathering nuts, berries, fruits, leaves, and herbs. For everything they harvested, most tribes would offer thanks and gratitude toward each plant and animal, and they were treated with respect and appreciation. Maybe we need to go back in time and reestablish old methods.

Moving on, how about the fact that animal rescues are in existence only because there are those among us who abuse the animals whose care we are charged with? Some of my dearest friends are in the business of rescuing animals that have been abandoned, starved, abused, beaten, and neglected until the beauty they possess is barely recognizable. I have seen horses with sunken sides, each rib countable, hip points prominently displayed, and, saddest of all, that look of being ready to give up on life pasted upon their faces. This look is not unique to the equine species but can be seen on the faces of many animals that end up in rescues through no fault of their own. The look of resignation is sad to witness and absolutely heartbreaking.

If this were done to you, how would you feel toward those who did it to you? What would you tell your herd, pack, or flock mates about the treatment you received? I have a feeling I know. I have also witnessed, many times, the successful rehabilitation of these abused animals. I don't think there is any animal that shows love and appreciation more than one that has been rescued from what would be a sure and slow death and given a second chance. I applaud those bighearted people who cannot say no to an animal in need.

We have those among us who make animals fight to the death for their pleasure. They also take free dogs and cats to use as bait animals. Those animals are killed by the others being trained to fight. We raise hogs for pork consumption where the sows live their lives in cages so small they cannot rise or turn around. The same is done to chickens raised to lay eggs for human consumption. They live their whole lives in a cage not big enough to turn around in. Or how about calves that are raised for veal? They are usually male calves from dairy herds that are considered unwanted and certainly not needed by dairy farmers. They are removed from their mother's care at birth and placed in a small cage until it is time to slaughter them for their meat. How much of a life were they allowed to experience? Not much, I'd guess.

Do you wear makeup or any other consumable products that you put on your face, hair, or body? Do you use pesticides or fertilizers? How about drugs for the many illnesses we humans experience? What about cleaning products for your home? How do you think companies came about getting approval for use of their products by humans? Unless you specifically search for products that exclude animals in their research, then you are consuming products that used animals to test their products for safety. Read an article by the Humane Society (Blog Spot/ Humane Society/ 2019/03)[1] and discover what their undercover investigation revealed.

Which animals are most commonly used to test products? In descending order from most used to least (according to the Humane Society of the US Blog 2019/03)[2], they are mice, rats, birds, rabbits, guinea pigs, hamsters, dogs, primates, and cats. The things they are subjected to can be horrific to say the least. Many of these animals are specifically bred and raised for research alone, and many will die during the research process or be euthanized afterward. That means they will never experience the feel of the wind on their faces or grass under their feet, be able to run and play with others of their tribe, experience snow on their tongues, or a do great many other things we take for granted.

What kind of life have we, as their stewards, provided for those animals, and why can't we understand they could be angered by the treatment they receive and possibly strike out against humans? It should not surprise you there are good and evil members in all species. We fail to see them as sentient beings simply because they do not speak to us out loud and in human languages. We demand so much proof, yet it is our failings that keep us from seeing what is reality. Animals? All they want is our company and to be seen as ones with much to teach. All animals, but especially animals domesticated by humans, deserve love, understanding, compassion, and care when needed. However, we walk around with this preconceived notion of how things are, all the while ignoring the magical world that lies right in front of us, awaiting our discovery.

Think about it the next time you look into the brown eyes of a beagle, one of the most popular of the dog breeds used for research. Before you look into those eyes, know this, the reason they use beagles in research: HSUS maintains in their resources (Humane Society/ Resources/Animals used in bio medical research 2020)[3] that beagles are used because they trust humans, are docile, and are of small stature. Now, go look into those eyes and know that by not voicing your outrage at the treatment they receive, you give silent approval of its continuance. Can you look into those brown, soulful eyes and feel good about yourself? I can, but only because I have spoken out and put my money where my mouth is. You can too.

I hope by telling the stories contained in this book, you have entertained the idea that maybe, just maybe, the animal kingdom is deeper than you thought and is worthy of reexamination—a reexamination where you see their intelligence, intuitiveness, and ability to communicate without words. To those who already believed, please see this as validation of your beliefs. Let's all go forward with a newfound knowledge about those who live behind the veil and treat them with the respect they have earned.

Just for today, let me see things as they truly are
and not as I have been led to believe.
Let me find peace in this exact moment
without giving energy to the past or future.
Let me find joy and release in tears
of laughter.

Let me live in a world of love and compassion
instead of worry and blame.
Just for today, let me change my direction
and learn to chart my future.

— R. D. Rowland

Footnotes

1. The Humane Society of the United States. "Animals used in biomedical research FAQ." Humane Society.org. [online] Available at: https://www.humanesociety. org/resources/animals-used-biomedical-research-faq [Accessed 14 March 2020].

2. The Humane Society of the United States. "What is the most commonly used species of animal in biomedical research?" The Humane Society.org [online] Available at: https://www.humanesociety.org/resources/animals-used-biomedical-research-faq#q2 [Accessed 14 March 2020].

3. Block, K., 2020. *"HSUS Undercover Investigation Shows Beagles Being Poisoned With Pesticides And Drugs, Killed At Animal Testing Lab."* [online]. A Humane World Kitty Blocks Blog. Available at: <https://blog.humanesociety.org/2019/03/ hsus-undercover-investigation-shows-beagles-being-poisoned-with-pesticides-and-drugs-killed-at-animal-testing-lab.html> [Accessed 14 March 2020].

About the Author

IN 2008, RICHARD WAS DIAGNOSED with a rare blood cancer called Multiple Myeloma, related to his time in Vietnam. At the time, he was given 3 years to live. Animals were the catalyst for change in his life. They were messengers, speaking of a universe previously unknown to him. They thinned the veil and allowed him to see what had been hidden. The lessons they taught led to his first published book, Unspoken Messages. That book led to other people telling Richard about their experiences with the animal kingdom, which birthed the idea for this book.

Richard is a two-tour veteran of the Vietnam war. He is retired from the Kentucky State Police after a twenty-eight-year career in law enforcement. He also owned and operated an equine boarding and training facility in his hometown of Elizabethtown, Kentucky for twenty years. His life has been spent in the company of animals. He strongly believes that animals and the peace their messages brought him are the reason he is still here today. They collectively removed fear from the journey.

CPSIA information can be obtained
at www.ICGtesting.com
Printed in the USA
LVHW040126131020
668648LV00002B/79